HOME PLATE

The Journey of the Most Flamboyant Father and Son Pitching Combination in Major League History

by

Steve Trout

with
Larry Names

The E. B. Houchin Company

est. 1992

The E.B. Houchin Company
5100 Daisy Lane
Murray, UT 84123

Copyright 2002 by Steve Trout

Hardcover ISBN: 0-938313-61-4
Trade Paperback ISBN: 0-938313-60-6

Library of Congress Number: 00-131907

For information, address inquiries to:
The E.B. Houchin Company
5100 Daisy Lane
Murray, UT 84123

First Printing: March 2002

Printed in USA

Table of Contents

Bradenton, Florida. Steve Trout attempts a comeback to the Majors. Encouragement from friends gets him a tryout with the Pittsburgh Pirates.

Biography of Paul "Dizzy" Trout, Steve's father, who was a Major League pitcher from 1939 to 1952. Recounts how Steve's parents met and married. Dizzy Trout's life after a Major League career.

Steve's family life growing up in a household with nine siblings. Beginnings of Steve's baseball life in Little League, then high school. Death of his father.

Steve is drafted by the Chicago White Sox. His minor league career. Marriage. Life in the minors. First Major League win. Being called up in mid-season. His career with the White Sox.

Steve is traded to the Chicago Cubs. The 1984 Cubs National League East Division. The 1984 NLCS. Troubles in the locker room. Traded to the New York Yankees in 1987.

Life in the Big Apple. Control problems. The Yankees in a pennant race. Nothing works in Yankee Stadium. Being stalked. Death threats. Life with George Steinbrenner.

Pre-Game Show

This book wasn't easy for me to write because it brings back memories of things I could have done differently. It has forced me to trace the footprints I once covered over.

After sharing my stories, experiences, and feelings with a close baseball friend, he said, "Steve, you should write a book." I chuckled. However, the idea simmered in the back of my mind.

Then a writer called from a local newspaper for an interview on the cross-town rivalry between the White Sox and Cubs. Having played for both teams, I was good copy. However, he soon became the interviewee. I asked him if he had ever written a book. He replied, "No." I then made him an offer to co-write my life story. He pondered, and I said, "I'll send you some writings and a cassette tape with stories, and if you like it, let's collaborate and do it."

Three years later we have this tremendous, insightful, revealing tale of the Trout family's life in baseball for much of the last 60 years.

Picking a title is always a gut wrenching experience because you know it's the first thing a person looks at, much the way we look at a beautiful woman or a handsome man. But to me *Home Plate* was it.

There was another title I liked, *My Innings, Carrying the Torch of a Famous Father in the Major Leagues*. *My Innings* was meant to exemplify the pressures that children have to carry when walking in the shadow of a famous parent. However, I knew *Home Plate* would be it because it has two meanings.

Growing up on the north side of Detroit in a big brick house, I remember the joys of big family get-togethers and the bountiful dinners we had. Relocating to Chicago and settling in South Holland, we moved into what had been St. Jude's convent, all decorated with a cross imbedded in the hallway and a praying altar in the basement. Dad would joke, "Heck, I'm the only Protestant you know that's living in a convent." I remember the great meals we shared there, too. The holidays were the best with 20 to 30 adults and lots of children running around and everyone enjoying the labors of my mother's and grandmother's culinary talents.

It was two special plates my mom made that contributed to my back-to-back shutouts in 1987 and my subsequent trade to the New York Yankees.

I was starting on a Thursday in Wrigley Field, so I stopped over to see Mom and asked her to make me her special hash brown potatoes. She used fresh chopped onions and mixed them into the grated potatoes with a little salt and pepper, then cooked them in a well seasoned cast-iron frying pan. They were great. I gave her a hug and a kiss and headed off to Clark and Addison. That game I pitched a shutout against the L.A. Dodgers without a burp.

I called Mom and said, "Let's do it again in four days. I got San Diego next."

Naturally, she pulled out the old cast-iron pan. Mom always said that the torch being held by the Statue of Liberty is not really a torch at all, that Lady Liberty is really holding up a frying pan. So this time I ate two plates of those succulent hash browns and headed for Wrigley. Once again, a beautiful shutout. Heck, I thought, maybe Mom was putting something extra in those hash browns. Unfortunately, I wouldn't have them anymore. I was traded the next day.

Looking back, maybe I should have taken Mom with me to New York. However, my six brothers and three sisters wouldn't have liked that.

Home Plate to me reveals my joys of a family, and it also symbolizes where my father and I made our livelihood. We live in a society today where families share very little time together at the dinner table, especially when many children are living in a single family homes. I feel dinner time is the most important thing a family can do together. Whether it's a single parent or a two-parent home, *Home Plate* is the most important.

Home Plate is also where the game of baseball starts and finishes, from the first pitch to the last. Once fans, like families, stop their appreciation of home plate, we, as a people, are destined to fall apart like a worn out baseball that has lost its seams.

To my Mother & Father,
my Grandparents,
my Brothers & Sisters,
and my special daughter Taytum
And special thanks to
the Cubs Grounds Crew
and Baseball Fans everywhere

Dizzy Trout
1915 - 1972

	1	2	3	4	5	6	7	8	9	R	H	E
Visitor	0											
Home	1											

Spring Training

Bradenton, Florida, February 28, 1997.
Had it really been that long already? Seven and a half years since I'd looked in for a slider sign, nodded okay, and pitched to a pro baseball player?

The rust fell away with the sweat on my forehead as I looked around the Pittsburgh Pirates training complex. A Mexico City team was waiting to take its cuts against me, a 39-year-old "comeback kid" trying my luck in spring training. They were eager to see how they'd do against a guy who'd carved out a 12-year career in the big leagues.

And me? I was just as eager to see how I'd do against them. A year earlier nobody would have bet a bag of old baseballs that I'd be throwing in a beer league, much less at a big league spring training camp. My career had staggered to a stop after the '89 season when I was 32. It was quite simply a mercy killing.

In 1987, when I was with the Yankees, one fateful inning against the White Sox changed me from one of the American League's toughest lefthanders into its most curious headcase. That day in Comiskey Park something just snapped in my mind, and soon my career was over. But more about that later.

There's no scientific name for what happened to me. I just couldn't throw the ball over the plate anymore.

This wasn't what baseball people call "control problems." That would have been a compliment. When I was on the mound, my heart and mind raced. My arm muscles tightened up like they were being twisted in a vise. The ball would soar over the umpire's head, bounce to the backstop, dive into the dirt; inside, outside, anywhere but in the strike zone. Nothing, not even therapy, helped me. I was a lost cause.

During spring training in 1990, baseball and I broke up. The decision was mutual.

For the next few years, I turned my focus to building a

baseball agency, finding young players and helping them find their way through the jungle of negotiations, equipment contracts, and minor league bus rides.

My road to Bradenton in 1997 started on an unlikely day in the summer of 1996, and in an unlikely place. That day my good friend Bill Bryk phoned me at my home in Munster, Indiana. Bryk was an Indiana-based scout for the Pirates at the time. Now he's an assistant to the general manager of the San Diego Padres. I've known him for years. He said he and a buddy, Dennis "Viva" Sepata, were driving to a park near my home to take some batting practice. Bill wondered if I'd be interested in throwing to them. I said sure because my 13-year-old daughter Taytum was visiting and she'd never seen her dad and his friends play some ball.

Taytum and I jumped into my Toyota and arrived at a parking lot near the field a few minutes later. The only trouble was, it was the wrong parking lot. Bill was parked on the other side of the park. So we had a decision to make: drive all the way around the park or through it. We met Bill and Dennis outside the ballpark fence a few minutes later.

"I knew it was you," said Bill, "when I saw you driving over the grass."

Inside the fence was a beautiful baseball diamond with well cut grass and a dragged infield. But the gates were locked. Not to be denied, we started to hop the fence.

Then a security guard yelled out, "Hey, the park is closed."

I yelled back, "He's a scout for the Pirates, and I'm a former Major League pitcher, and this guy is an attorney. I think we qualify to play here."

He left us alone.

We flung bats and balls over the fence. "Viva" climbed the fence with no problem, then Bill asked him to hold a steel can for him. The can, which was about the size of a bread box, went over the fence, but as Bill made the climb, he got stuck. One leg hung over one side, the other leg over the other side. As "Viva" and I helped him over, Taytum chuckled at these three "old" guys struggling over a fence to show off their baseball talents.

"Viva" decided he'd start at the plate, hitting off Bill. I shagged balls in center field. My arm felt good as I threw balls, nice and easy, back to the infield. Finally, I let one go toward home plate, and it went all the way in — on the fly.

Bill's eyes shot over to me. "What was that?" he said.

I looked at my arm and said, "What was that?"

2

I moved in to the mound and began throwing batting practice. It was just me, my daughter, and a couple of buddies, and my mind was clear as a mountain stream. I threw, and they took their swings. After a while, Bill went to the steel can. Inside was his trusty friend: his radar gun. He pulled it out, just out of curiosity. My next pitch, he pointed the gun at me, and sure enough, I was throwing 88 miles per hour. That wasn't bad, especially for a guy who'd been out of the Majors for seven years.

Bill was more excited than I was. "Why don't you throw in a few days and see if you're still throwing hard," he said.

So I did.

A couple of days later, I went to scout a small college game outside Chicago: Thornton vs. Xavier. Bill suggested I go to the bullpen during the game and make a few throws. One of the kids from Thornton was in the bullpen with me, and as I started to heat up, he stopped to watch. Bill aimed his gun, and it registered upper-80s again.

"Steve," Bill said, "you've got to make a comeback."

"Bullshit," I said. "I'm going to throw 90 this time."

I was in the moment. After the next pitch, Bill shouted so loud I thought they'd stop the game. "Here it is! Here it is! Here it is! He threw 90! He threw 90!" As we walked off the field, he showed me the gun. Sure enough, it said 90.

"You *have* to make a comeback," he said. Then, in case I'd missed it the first time, he said, "You *have* to make a comeback. We only have one lefty in the whole organization who's throwing in the 90s."

At that point, I didn't know what to think.

After a brief spring training stint with the St. Louis Cardinals in 1990, baseball and I split, and until this time in '97, I hadn't given much thought to playing again. I'd built up a clientele as a player agent, and the game had become a recreational release for me instead of a job. A couple of years before I'd been pitching coach for the Merrillville Muddogs, an independent minor league team in the area. But that was a casual baseball job at best. The team folded after just one season, and since then, my dalliances with the game had been for pleasure only — some afternoon throwing and batting practice with Bill and other friends.

But Bill was serious. The radar gun doesn't lie, and I could tell by the way Bill was talking that he meant business.

I believe what Bill says because baseball wasn't the only thread between us. Bill and I have a spiritual sixth sense — things we've both felt or seen that lead us to believe larger forces are at work in our lives.

Bill had a daughter, too. Becky was seven years old when she died of leukemia. One day, when his daughter was still alive, Bill was standing in his backyard near the house. Some shingles tore loose from the roof and fell near him. Becky made a cross out of the strips of shingles and said, "God loves you." She died shortly after that, and Bill said after her death that he began to feel more in touch with his spiritual side, that he still felt her presence, and that her spirit was somewhere watching over him.

One time he was driving to Florida and got caught in heavy fog. He pulled over suddenly, desperately sad, and grieved over Becky. He prayed, and as the fog lifted and it became clear, he felt he had connected with her spirit. He recently found the cross she had made, and now it hangs proudly in his home.

My mother, Pearl, passed away on, of all days, Pearl Harbor Day, 1994. My nine brothers and sisters and I still miss her dearly. She was a remarkable woman, the glue that held us to-gether as a family. She was a best friend to each of us.

And now, Bill felt my mother was connecting with my spirit. "Steve, I believe this is a calling for you," he said. "I think there's an angel on your shoulder who wants you to come back and get rid of whatever happened before. Your mother is giving you the strength. Her spirit is with you, and your mom wants you to come back to baseball."

More than anything else, that's what convinced me to go to Florida for spring training. My mom was saddened by the way my career had ended. She never said so, but I could sense that was what she was feeling.

The more I thought about what Bill had said, the more I thought maybe he was right. I felt I had more of my mom's strength with me, a feeling that maybe she was still supporting me, only in a different way. Even though she's gone, she could still look over all 10 of her kids and be a guardian in a way she couldn't when she was alive. It's more that we sense her spirit, the way she was as a loving mother. There's a saying: "The older you get, the smarter your father becomes." I feel we are more in tune with her now than when she was alive. I somehow feel that way.

So that's how I ended up a 39-year-old at spring training.

Upon arriving in Florida, I loaded my newfound strength and self-confidence into a $170-a-week car from Rent-A-Dent, a white Mercury four-door that often didn't start. The investment in rickety wheels was no accident. It was a psychological ploy, my attempt to put a former million-dollar pitcher into a minor league frame of mind. I didn't need anyone from the Pirates telling me, "You haven't done anything lately." My car reminded me of that every time I turned the ignition. I was going to spring training the same way I had as a 19-year-old rookie.

When I arrived at camp, I was the source of curiosity. All the Pirates coaches and front office had to go on was the recommend-ation of Bill Bryk, some radar numbers, and the stats from my 12-year Major League career, which included a 4.18 career ERA — a number that in 1997 could draw a three-year contract for at least $3 million per.

How 20 years can change a man. Instead of just arriving right on time for camp, as I did during my prime, I showed up a few days early. I knew that settling into the locker room and the Bradenton, Florida facility would help create a comfort zone and be one less distraction when it came time to pitch.

Pulling the jersey over my head and shoving my right hand into the glove wasn't as daunting as I'd thought it might be. As I ran and stretched out, I didn't think about that fateful day as a Yankee in 1987 when I threw between-inning warmup pitches all over Comiskey Park and short-circuited my career. Instead, my thoughts were of the pleasure of running on cut green grass under a warm Florida sun.

My time away seemed more like eight months than almost eight years. Little by little, I began to blend in. Jon Lieber, one of the Pirates pitchers, who is now with the Cubs and enjoying a three-year contract, came up to me to find out what my story was, and when I told him, he said, "This is a good thing. That's great." One of the first basemen came up to say hi. They were typical of the people who approached me: pleasant and enthusiastic.

But there were others who weren't, who mumbled under their breath that I had no business there, that I was probably broke and looking for money. They didn't matter. I knew I was doing the right thing, for the right reasons, and nobody else needed to know.

Not only did my mind feel right, my arm did, too. Yes, there were times if I was playing catch and threw the ball improperly, I'd get some tension in my arm. And when I did, the thoughts of my New York nightmare did a Texas two-step in the back of my head. But I combated those bad vibes with the feeling I had in-side. "I'm so happy to be here," I told myself. "I'm supposed to be here. This is my decision to be here, not baseball's."

The first few days of camp, the radar gun confirmed as much. I was supposed to be there. They clocked me as fast as 92 miles per hour. The coaches said my slider was one of the hardest they'd seen in a long time from a left-hander. I could have told them to expect that. When I pitched in the Majors from 1978 to 1989, left-handed hitters knew that when Steve Trout was on, his slider could leave them swinging like a rusty gate. Reggie Jackson once said I was one of the toughest left-handers he'd ever faced.

But now I had to prove myself all over again against this Mexican team. Bill Bryk was standing there, his trusty radar gun at his side, and there were 30 Pirates people hanging around, as well as coaches and front office people, including general manager Cam Bonifay.

My warm-up pitches felt great, and velocity was good. The best part was that my warm-up pitches hit the catcher's glove. A good sign. The first Mexican hitter walked to the plate. I was hoping for the best, thinking, "Is this a new beginning or a continuation of the past?" The lead-off hitter was looking at this big gringo and hoping for the best also. I peered in for the signs, and I saw the Pirates management peering back at me. My history and the history I inherited from my dad were on the line. I could feel the feedback, their questions, "Why is Trout here? What does he hope to get out of this?"

I was asking myself the same questions.

	1	2	3	4	5	6	7	8	9	R	H	E
Visitor	0	0										
Home	1	0										

Dizzy

If a woman in Detroit hadn't baked a chocolate cake, I might not be here today. But that's getting ahead of the story.

My dad, Paul "Dizzy" Trout, was born June 29, 1915, in Sandcut, a tiny farm community in southwestern Indiana. His father worked the land as a tenant farmer, and Dad spent much of his childhood hopping from one Indiana backroad to another, to places with names like Ehrmandale and New Goshen and Cider City. People in that part of Indiana say that, if Dad could find something that fit into his hand, he'd throw it. He'd pick up an orange and see how far he could throw it, or he'd gather walnuts and see if he could knock a squirrel out of a tree.

When he was 13, his mother Emma died from natural causes, and some time later his father married Christine Decker, a woman my father never liked. Christine was later admitted to a mental institution and her five children, my dad's half-brothers and half-sisters, were sent to an orphanage and remained there until the required age of 18. One of them, Uncle Don, owns a car dealership in Lafayette, Indiana. From that day onward, Dad always said, he was an orphan. When Dad met Mom and her family, he told them both his parents were dead. Later, after they were married, he told the truth, that his father was alive and had remarried. My dad loved his mother Emma so much that, when his father said his new wife was the only woman he ever loved, Dad was hurt so bad that he went off to earn a living playing ball without graduating from high school. At an early age, he decided that, if he was going to make it in this world, then he'd have to rely mostly on himself. And that he did.

One hot afternoon as a teenager, he was out hoeing corn with his cousin, who happened to share a name with a future Major League star named Frank Howard. As they hoed, Dad stopped to

7

wipe the sweat off his head, looked into the blazing sun, and proclaimed to Frank, "Surely, there is a better way of life." It wasn't long afterward that he left his father and stepmother and set off to be a baseball player.

Dad started out playing baseball as a kid, and in those days, if you could hit, throw, and run, a team would find you, even in a one-horse town like Sandcut. In 1935, when he was 19 years old, he broke into pro ball with a team called the Terre Haute Tots. Because of his age and lack of transportation to games, he would hitch a ride on a melon truck. People used to tell us that he would limber up his arm the same way he did as a kid, by throwing whatever was handy. In this case, it was some of the smaller honeydew melons on the way into the big city.

On the mound, Dad was a picture of intensity. He filled out to nearly six-foot-three and 195 pounds, which in those days cut an imposing figure on the mound. And not only did he have stuff, he had style. In the back pocket of his uniform flannels, he always stuffed a red, decorated handkerchief — which he used only when he played with the Toledo Mudhens. When he got to the big leagues, they told him to leave the red handkerchief at home because the team thought that was showboating. Dad continued to have the handkerchief in his back pocket. It was his trademark, but he respected the team's wishes and pulled it out just once in a while.

The red handkerchief was so well-known it led to one of the funniest happenings in Tiger baseball history. Every summer the Tigers put on Amateur Day at Briggs Stadium. In 1947 Dizzy Trout had been mopping up other teams, and also mopping up his sweaty brow with his famous huge red handkerchief.

That summer at the 31st Amateur Day game two of the locals, Jimmy Basta and Bobby Hoeft, both of whom would sign with Major League teams that same fall, decided to have some fun.

When Hoeft came to bat for the first time, he stepped into the box, then immediately called time out. He reached into his hip pocket and removed a huge red handkerchief and proceeded to wipe his sweaty brow. As more than 20,000 spectators roared in laughter, Hoeft stepped back into the box.

As Jimmy Basta was about to deliver his first pitch, *he* called time, stepped off the mound and pulled out *his* red handkerchief and wiped away his own sweat. The crowd was in hysterics, and each one there was thinking of one person: the much-loved, colorful Dizzy Trout.

8

Everyone came to know that Trout pitched the same way he lived. No bull, straight at you, just lay what you've got on the table and let's see what happens. Some pitchers would hem and haw, shake off signs, pretend to doctor the ball — anything to distract the hitter. Not Dad. He'd come at you low and hard with his fastball. If you could hit it, you were the better man. If you couldn't, he was. No questions asked. The outfielders Dad played with have been known to say they liked it when he pitched because he worked fast and they knew the game would be short.

In those days, just like it is today, making the Major Leagues was a huge accomplishment. With only eight teams in each league, a roster spot in "The Show" was a cause for celebration. Then came the real battle, staying there.

Naturally, the Major Leagues were the pinnacle back then, but the minors were the heartbeat. You could barely drive a hundred miles without finding a farm team of some level, from "Triple -A" all the way down to "D" and "E" ball. When Major League teams signed players, they often farmed them out to minor league clubs and waited for the cream to rise to the top. Most guys in Dad's era were signed by lower level minor league teams, and if they were any good, teams at a higher level would buy their contracts. By this process, players would gradually make it to the Majors. Most players never made it. Those who did reach the top got there much later in their careers than ballplayers do today. Sending a 26-year-old rookie to the plate for his first Major League at-bat was not unusual. Today, it's a much different story. Most young players who are drafted and signed for a substantial bonus are accelerated through the minors to the Majors at early ages, simply to justify the money the organization gave them. Bonus money was not part of my dad's era.

As for my dad, the Detroit Tigers plucked him from semi-pro ball and sent him to the minors. Along the way, he earned MVP of the Texas League in 1938 and finally got the call from the big team in the 1939 season, when he would turn 24.

In 1938, the Tigers had been a better than average team. They finished 84-70, fourth in the American League. Heading into 1939, the sportswriters were looking for some stories about the new blood coming up to the team. Hal Newhouser, a pitcher who broke in the same year as Dad, was one of them. Dad was another; he was good newspaper copy waiting to be written.

Dad was known as a real character when he was in the minors. His nickname, Dizzy, as the story goes, dates to those days.

One game, when it was raining cats and dogs, the umpire called time and sent the teams to their dugouts. Dad, always looking for something different, saw an awning hanging in center field. He figured he'd just run out there and stand under the awning until the rain passed. After he ran all the way out there, he saw that the awning wasn't real. It had been painted on the wall. Everyone thought this was the funniest thing they had ever seen, and so they called him Dizzy, or Diz for short, from then on.

The name stuck because it fit. Dad was always joking with his teammates, playing practical jokes or hamming it up with the sportswriters. When the Tigers finally called his number, the newspapers picked up on his eccentric side right away. It was an easy score, so they sent a photographer out to the ballpark to take a picture of the Tigers' new rookie prankster.

It didn't hurt that the other Dizzy, Dizzy Dean of the Cardinals, was nearing the end of his career, and the writers were looking for another player who could equal Dean's antics and off-the-wall personality. They got one in my dad. On the mound and off the field, he was as serious as a librarian. But the rest of the time, and especially at the park, he was the team cut-up. One newspaper photographer snapped a shot that embodied his silly side to perfection. In the photo, his hat is cocked on his head, not the way a catcher or a position player would wear it, but kind of in between. It hangs over his right ear like a pot handle. On the left side, his ear sticks out from under the cap like a plane flap. His smiling cheeks are squeezing his eyes into tiny slits. He's wearing the script "Detroit" on his chest and a squinty-eyed farm-boy grin on his face.

When he joined the Tigers, it didn't take long for him to show he was going to have some fun. On one of Dad's first days with the team in spring training down in Florida, Tigers manager Mickey Cochrane strolled into the hotel and stopped suddenly when he noticed some of his players mingling in the corner. They were hanging out with a hayseed stranger who had buck teeth, a wig, ill-fitting clothes, and a flaming red bandana tied around his neck.

"Who's that?" Cochrane asked one of his veterans.

"That's one of your rookie pitchers — Trout," the player replied.

Cochrane grunted back, "If he can win ball games, then he can dress up like Santa Claus and it will be all right with me. But if he can't pitch winning ball, then he'd better get rid of the masquerade stuff in a hurry."

A few days later at camp, a policeman from nearby Lakeland stopped by at the Tigers workout on his motorcycle. Dad thought the bike was a riot, and asked if he could borrow it for a tour around the park. The fans and players laughed out loud as Dad drove around the warning track and the infield, then wove in and out of practice groups. Soon, Cochrane appeared on the dugout steps. As Dad passed, he waved at his skipper and shouted, "How'm I doing, Mick?"

Cochrane shot Dad a look that could kill and yelled back, "Fine — and keep right on riding until you get to Toledo. That's where you'll be on Opening Day!"

As it turned out, he did end up in Toledo that opening day. But he'd be back. And that's where the chocolate cake comes in.

One day in February 1939, a 19-year-old Detroit woman named Ruth Ortmann was listening to a broadcast about the up-and-coming Tigers as spring training approached. Ruth said to her older sister, Pearl, "That Paul Trout sounds like a lot of fun. He has a duck for a pet." Ruth continued. "Maybe I'll write him a fan letter."

Pearl said, "I don't care."

Ruth replied, "I've got an idea. I'll tell him I'll bake him a cake or a pie for every game he wins this season. What do you think?"

Pearl, reading a book, answered. "I don't care."

So, Ruth wrote a letter and sent it to Paul Trout in Lakeland, Florida, promising him a cake or pie for every game he won that season. No reply to her letter was forthcoming, and soon the Tigers opened the season in Cleveland. Ruth wondered if Paul Trout would ever answer her letter. She said to Pearl, "Maybe I should write him again. Maybe he lost our address. What do you think, Pearl?"

Again, Pearl said, "I don't care."

Ruth wrote one more time and told Paul that she wouldn't bother him again if he didn't reply. Lo and behold, he did write a response. He wrote that he'd like a chocolate cake with nuts and that he hoped he'd keep her busy baking all season. He let her know that he was staying at the Leland Hotel in Detroit with Schoolboy Rowe and Fred Hutchinson and that they'd sure enjoy the cake. If she wanted tickets, she should call him at the hotel.

Every time Dad pitched, Ruth would have all the ingredients ready to bake the cake. She had to put all the ingredients back many times until May 24, 1939, when Paul won a game. Ruth baked him the chocolate cake with nuts. She and her father, Arno Ortmann, took the cake to the Leland Hotel, the cake resting in a hat box. She went to the front desk and said, "This is for Paul Trout."

The clerk gave her a big smile and said, "Would you like to call his room?" He handed Ruth the phone.

She stood there, nervously wondering what she'd say if he answered.

Dad wasn't there. Ruth was relieved. She gave the phone back to the clerk and left the cake with him to deliver to Dad.

The next day in the sports pages under a column titled, *Tiger Tales*, the headline read:

TROUT TAKES THE CAKE
Paul Trout has a fan who baked him a cake for his win.

Dad brought the cake into the Tigers clubhouse, and Charlie Gehringer said, after a big bite, "Diz, you ought to marry that gal."

The next day Ruth and her father went to the game. While sitting in the stands waiting for the crowd to leave after the game, they saw Dad walk by in his street clothes, and Ruth said, "That's him! That's Paul Trout." Dressed in a light-green suit, he impressed Ruth with his broad shoulders. She introduced herself. "Hi, I'm Ruth Ortmann."

Dad said, "It's nice to meet you. I said for you to call me for tickets." Then he mentioned he was in a hurry and continued walking to the parking lot.

Shortly after that, Ruth went to another game, and this time she brought Pearl with her. They decided to wait for Dad outside the locker room and say hi to him again. Then he stopped to talk.

"Well, who did you bring this time?" he said.

"This is my sister, Pearl," said Ruth.

For the next 15 minutes, all Ruth saw was the back of my dad's head, after he set eyes on Pearl.

When they all parted, Ruth knew that something special had happened. "He liked you, Pearl," she said, but her older sister denied it all the way home.

One week later they invited him over for dinner. They talked no baseball, and Dad didn't drink too much beer, just the right amount. As soon as dinner was over, they went into the living room to talk. As Dad was leaving the room, he tripped over the throw rug and said, "We don't have those in Indiana. We live on sand floors." For that reason, and others, the evening was memorable. The time had flown by, as if Dad had been part of the family his whole life. Everybody knew, though, that his affections were all for Pearl.

Aunt Ruth loves to tell this story because, even though she was the one who wrote the letter and baked the cake, she never felt jealous when Dad and Mom tied the knot, something we — her nieces and nephews — thank her for all the time. She never developed a crush on my dad. Their relationship was always friendship and appreciation, and both knew that my mom was really the one he was interested in. Even today, the fact Aunt Ruth was the one who introduced them is a source of great pride and pleasure for her.

It was love at first sight for Mom and Dad. Aunt Ruth says she knew he was head over heels when he started writing Mom letters from the road. On their first date, he borrowed a car from a bellhop at the hotel and drove her around town. Mom had never had a serious boyfriend, and on their first night out together, he drove her through the best neighborhoods of Detroit, looking at the scenery and the houses where Henry Ford and other high-profile people lived. At one point, Dad pointed out the window and said, "Someday, we're going to live in a house like that." He proposed on their first date. Pearl could scarcely believe it. Here she barely knew this guy and already he was talking about houses and marriage. But Dad knew he had found his true love. Already, he was walking around the clubhouse telling the guys, "You know, I think I've found the girl I want to marry."

True enough, six weeks later, on September 27, 1939, they were married, and a few years later they ended up in a house just like the one he had pointed at on their first date.

During the early years of their marriage, they lived with my mother's parents, who incidentally lived with our family later on in their lives until their deaths in 1976 and 1982.

For the rest of his baseball career, Dad was very productive — on and off the mound. We have 10 children in our family, seven boys and three girls. When Dad would hit the banquet circuit (some people called it the "chicken circuit" because you were almost always guaranteed to be served chicken) people would ask him if he was Catholic. He would reply in his Indiana drawl, "I'd be Catholic if I could afford it. Heck, I'm just a passionate Protestant."

When World War II hit, the Tigers, like other teams, lost some of their best players to war. Hank Greenberg became a soldier in 1941 and didn't return to baseball until July of 1945. My dad, on account of his less-than-perfect eyesight, stayed home. After going 9-9 in 1941 and 12-18 the following season, he finally got it together in 1943. Dad won a league-high 20 games and lost just 12 that season. He followed that up with 27-14 in '44, 18-15 in '45 and 17-12 in '46, the year he made $25,000. Hal Newhouser evolved into the other half of the Tigers one-two punch. He won 29 games in 1944, then 25 and 26 the next two seasons.

The record books show that Dizzy Trout went 1-1 in the 1945 World Series, posting a 0.66 ERA and helping the Tigers beat the Cubs. Because of the war, many people remember that Series as a sloppily played one, with each roster sporting its share of over-the-hill veterans and sub-par war-time talent. (By the way, the Cubs haven't been back to the Fall Classic since.) Dad stayed with the Tigers until 1952, when he limped to a 1-5 start and was traded to the Red Sox. He appeared in 26 games with Boston, finishing 9-8. After that season, at the age of 37, he was forced to call it quits. Bill Veeck, then trying to buy the Orioles, helped him get a brief comeback shot in 1957, when I was six weeks old, but it didn't work out.

One of the more sentimental moments of my career was when I took the mound in Baltimore in 1982, where the marquee sign in center field read:

**ON SEP 11 1957 HERE THE LATE PAUL
'DIZZY' TROUT PITCHED HIS LAST BIG
LEAGUE GAME - - FOR THE O'S VS KC
AT THAT TIME HIS SON STEVE WAS
6 WEEKS OLD
HE IS THE SAME STEVE TROUT
STARTING FOR THE WHITE SOX TONIGHT**

I didn't even see that sign. I pitched a two-hitter, and a week later, a fan sent me a picture that had me in the foreground and the sign in the background. Fans, like this one, are good for the game. This person did something nice for me and asked for nothing in return. These are the kind of fans we play for.

That, in a nutshell, was Dad's career. Dizzy Trout was solid as a rock when it came to the important things in life, but he was as unpredictable as a Kansas summer when it came to having fun.

Looking back on it, he really had some career. He won 170 games, and in '44, Dad and Newhouser broke the Major League record for most wins in a season by two teammates with 56. Both are acknowledged as two of the top 10 pitchers in the history of the Detroit Tigers.

In 1944 Dad topped the rest of the American League pitchers with an ERA of only 2.12. Dad finished second in the Cy Young voting two years in a row, 1943-44. The winner in '44 was Hal Newhouser, beating out Dad by only four votes. That same year Dad was selected for the American League All-star team. He also led the league with 33 complete games and threw seven shutouts. It's hard to imagine any pitcher in baseball today, who could match that kind of endurance.

Dizzy Trout could also hit the ball. He is eleventh on the all-time list for home runs by a pitcher.

The '45 World Series was one of the highlights of my dad's career. He beat the Cubs in game 4, throwing a five-hitter and giving up just one run, unearned. In game 6 Dad came on in relief in the eighth with the score tied, 7-7. In the bottom of the 12th, the score still tied with two outs, Stan Hack hit a drive to left field that landed in front of Hank Greenberg. The ball bounded over Greenberg all the way to the wall, and the winning run scored from first base. It was later determined that the ball had hit a sprinkler head, but Dad wasn't buying that, and had more than a few choice words for Greenberg as he came into the dugout.

Dad finished his career 170-161 with a 3.23 ERA, although some people say that he made his career against guys who weren't healthy enough to fight in the war. But I know he would have been a good pitcher at any time, anywhere — in the '70s or '80s or whenever. He had abilities and a respect for baseball that made him one of the fiercest competitors in the game. Ted Williams will tell you my dad was one of his most challenging foes.

The Detroit Tigers have Dad on their all-time team, and he is in the Indiana Baseball Hall of Fame. So far Dizzy Trout has not been given his place in the Hall of Fame at Cooperstown, but I am sure I am not the only one who believes he belongs there.

Like a lot of guys who played back then, Dad didn't make a lot of guys who played back then, Dad didn't make a lot of money. In those days, contracts were year-to-year, and the owners had all the power. Dad went in for his negotiations after the 1945 season when he won 18 games. The Tigers said they didn't want to give him a raise because he'd had a worse year than he did in

1944 when he won 27. A few years ago I found the contract he signed back then, and Mom told me the story about how Dad was found in the Tigers offices one afternoon, chasing the general manager around the desk, screaming, "Goddammit! I've got another kid to keep shitting!" That was his country way of saying he had another kid on the way, another mouth to feed. I think he got the raise. Later, the Tigers promised him a lifetime job with the team, but they never came through on it. They tried to put him on the radio, but Dad always shot straight from the hip, and I don't know if they liked that. The other announcer, Van Patrick, read all the beer commercials. During one game, Dad said, "Hell, I should be doing the beer commercials! I'm the one who drinks the stuff." Although Dad's radio work was becoming very well liked, Patrick felt Dad's color commentating was getting too popular, so they agreed on a break-up.

With no baseball opportunities available, Dad did whatever it took to provide for us. He worked as a salesman, an announcer, a bartender. My brother Paul remembers my dad, a large-framed, big-shouldered former star of the Tigers, competing for a sheet metal job with a bunch of pencil-necked men. He did what had to be done, and I admire him for that. All he was interested in was going to work and providing for the family, and I think it was through this struggle that he really learned about himself as a man. He had self-assurance, confidence, and a strong base of friends.

One day in our living room we were watching home movies, and one scene showed Dad on a fishing trip with his buddies. The next scene showed Mom at home with the kids climbing all over her. The scene after that showed Dad on a hunting trip with all his friends on an island in Michigan, followed by a scene with Mom in the backyard with the kids. The laundry was in the background, waiting to be hung up, and the kids were climbing all over her again. Then it showed Dad in Europe on a baseball trip. All of a sudden, Mom said to the eight of us watching this, "Turn this off. This is really pissing me off!" We all laughed because that was Mom's sense of humor.

When one of those friends, his old Orioles buddy Bill Veeck, finally came into control of the White Sox, we moved to Chicago so Dad could work for him. It was 1961, and we looked like Ma and Pa Kettle with their brood of 10 kids. Our house had once been St. Jude's Convent. It was the only house that could hold everybody and everything we had. The brick home didn't look large from the outside, but inside, it went on and on, a maze of one room after another. It came complete with a cross designed into the tile in the front foyer, and a miniature altar in the basement. "I'm the only Protestant you know who lives in a convent," Dad used to tell people. All the kids are grown and on their own now, and I always wanted to burn the house down rather than endure the pain of seeing someone else live in it. But in January of 1999 my brother sold it.

The White Sox hired Dad as a public relations man. He would organize banquets and run promotions at Comiskey Park. Jerome Holtzman, the longtime baseball writer for *The Chicago Tribune*, who's in the Hall of Fame himself, told me that my dad's bark was worse than his bite, unless you tried to dig in on him, then he would knock you on your ass. Tigers Hall of Famer Al Kaline, who had the shortest autograph in baseball (Al K—), once told me that one day, Larry Doby yelled at my dad from the on-deck circle. When Doby, an eventual Hall of Famer himself, came up to bat, the first pitch hit him in the back. If Dad didn't like something you did or said, he'd address it with you and settle it. One time at the ballpark, a fan was heckling Dad unmercifully. He ignored it for awhile. Then recognizing the heckler as an employee of the team, he went over to the box seat and grabbed the guy by the collar and pulled him toward him. After realizing the heckler was in a wheelchair, he sat him down and asked the man why he was heckling him, especially since he was an employee. Unfortunately, a photographer from *Life* magazine took pictures and caught the frustration on Dad's face as he addressed the heckler. Dad felt horrible about this because his lack of control had gotten the best of him.

But Dad really had a compassionate heart. He was demanding and wanted things to be done right, but he was soft inside, which explains all of the charity work that he did.

In the early 1960s, Dad and George Allen, the former NFL head coach, went to South Dakota to bring gifts and sports equipment to the children at Pine Ridge Indian Reservation. After returning home, they started the Red Cloud Sports Banquet, which still raises money for the children on the reservation. The Sioux people were so grateful to Dad that they officially cut the ribbon in 1974 on the new Paul "Dizzy" Trout Memorial Fieldhouse.

"My father has not been forgotten by the baseball people as every year I'm asked to present the Paul "Dizzy" Trout Award at the Pitch & Hit Banquet held in Chicago. The committee selects someone from the baseball world who is making a major contribution to the game. I make it a point to be there every year because I am so honored that my father is still so loved by his baseball friends. This event is held in January.

In 1997, Dave Dombrowski, who is the general manager of the Florida Marlins, was the recipient of the award. Before the presentation, I normally make a short speech. I mentioned a few things about Dave and how he got started in the front office about the same time I was starting to pitch for the White Sox. I ended the speech by saying, "You know what they say about Miami, that the nicest thing about Miami is that it's close to the United States." A few people got the joke, then I went on to say, "But now that Dave Dombrowski is the general manager of the Florida Marlins, I believe the nicest thing they're going to say about Miami is that they won the World Series." This was quite a prediction. Lo and behold! The Marlins went on and won the World Series that year.

The following year the award went to Roland Hemond of the Arizona Diamondbacks. He was the general manager with the Sox when I was drafted in 1976. Roland has been a family friend for over 30 years and is one of the most respected executives in baseball.

As I presented the award to Roland, I reminded him of my psychic powers and said, "I hope this award is a good luck charm for you like it was for the Marlins." The next day Roland called to thank me for the kind words and invited me to have dinner with him before returning to Arizona. The D-backs didn't win the World Series that year because it was their first year in the National League, but they did win their division the following year.

Dad's St. Jude Sports Nights, where he would land the biggest names in sports as guest speakers each year, became an institution in the south suburbs of Chicago. Dad lacked a formal education, but he was a very smart man. He never had public speaking classes, yet he was a gifted speaker. I don't have the faintest idea how he did it. When Dad was organizing a banquet, stars like Bobby Hull of the Blackhawks and Tommy John of the White Sox came — not because they had to, but because Dizzy Trout had asked them. Today, I hear people say, "Oh, your dad had us falling in the aisles laughing. He was a great storyteller and comedian, and he had such a natural style." I think it was because he feared nothing. He never questioned himself. He wasn't there to convert people to anything. He was just being himself.

My dad was respected by just about everyone he met, a fact I am reminded of often. One particular encounter I had with a former Major Leaguer in Florida a few years ago will always stay with me.

My buddy, Mike McDonald, and I were fishing in a place called Islamorada in the Florida Keys. We were on a week-long fishing vacation and driving around looking for a place to have a beer, when we pulled up to a stoplight and started looking around. Mike spotted a Chevy Suburban next to us and said, "Look, it's Ted Williams!"

"Roll down the window!" I yelled, looking over at Mike. "Roll down the window!"

I couldn't wait any longer. So I hopped out of the car, ran over to the passenger side of the Suburban and knocked on the window. Inside sat Ted Williams, the greatest hitter of all time. He rolled down his passenger-side window about three inches. I said, "I'm Steve Trout, Dizzy's son!"

He said, "Hey! Hey, listen up! I'm the last house at the end of the road. I'll be there in 10 minutes."

It took us three, and there we were at Ted Williams' home. We waited in his front yard, with his dogs barking and trying to sniff out who was in this strange car.

Five minutes later, Ted showed up. He got out, and so did we. He greeted us with a mighty handshake, a product of a wrist and forearm that launched 2,654 hits during a career that was interrupted twice by war. The hospitality was sincere for the son of a former contemporary. When Ted and my dad played, the guys didn't worry about what kind of dough Nike was going to spot them or how much of a cut their agents were getting. They just went out and gave it all they had. They got their uniforms dirty, took a shower, tossed down a beer, and went home. The players respected each other, which was part of the reason that Ted Williams and Dizzy Trout came to know each other.

One time the Tigers and Red Sox were playing, and my dad was on the mound. The bases were loaded, and Ted came up to bat. Dad stepped off the mound and wiped his sweaty forehead off with that red handkerchief. Then he got back on the hill and worked the count to three balls, two strikes. Then he let fly with a fastball that rode in on Ted, who swung and missed. The young righty had struck out the best hitter in the game. Well, after that game, my dad was so excited that he went to see Ted in the locker room and asked him to sign the strikeout ball. Ted couldn't believe it. After all, these teams had just played a fierce game that Williams had lost by striking out, and now the guy who fanned him wanted the ball signed? Williams thought he was nuts. But he said, "If you're crazy enough to ask me to sign the ball, I'll sign it."

The next time they faced each other, the situation was the very same. Bases loaded, 3-2 count, game on the line. Dad wiped his forehead, thinking that what worked once just might work again. He threw the fastball, and this time Ted smacked it about nine miles over the fence. As Ted trotted around third base, he looked over his shoulder at my dad and yelled, "Hey, Dizzy, I'll sign that one too — if you can find it!"

Ted Williams and my dad faced each other many times. During one game Ted took a two-strike pitch for a called strike three. Being the aggressive hitter he was, Ted was rarely called out on strikes. He was so upset by the call he tossed his bat high in the air, and it landed thirty feet away. The Tiger manager, Red Rolfe, charged out of the dugout, demanding that Ted be ejected for the flagrant show of poor sportsmanship. Rolfe, for his efforts, was ejected instead.

Some years later a similar situation occurred. Ted had two strikes. The next pitch was clearly a strike, at least as far as Dad was concerned. Both he and the Tiger manager Fred Hutchinson strenuously argued the point to the plate umpire, but to no avail. Ted hit the next pitch for a game-winning double.

In 1952, in his final at-bat before leaving to fight in the Korean War, Ted Williams hit a game winning two-run HR to beat Dizzy Trout and the Tigers.

Ted and my dad were just like each other, fierce as foes and dear as friends. That's why Ted was eager to lead us into the house, which was filled with the smell of garlic and scampi. Ted gave us a couple of 16-ounce Budweisers and poured himself a full glass of gin and tonic. We sat in his living room just enjoying the moment, the warm breeze on the patio, and the company. We talked about the old-time game and how great it was as well as the players' pension, which was a hot topic with the older former players back then. Ted pulled out a pen and paper and drew graphs to explain what he was talking about, about how some of the great wartime ballplayers were privately suffering financially because of the terrible pension plans they played under. I agreed with him, and said that I'd be glad to contribute to the cause if we could find others who would.

I asked him, "What's the biggest difference between my dad's era versus my era?"

"It's the agents," he said. It was obvious this wasn't one of his favorite topics. When Ted hit .406 in 1941, he had 18 at-bats that in today's game would be considered sacrifices. If the rule about sacrifices existed back then, his average would have been up over .410. Ted's best year and Dad's best year would demand $10,000,000 or more today.

That night my friend Mike was in total awe. We tossed down a couple of big beers and ate some garlic scampi.

"We'll go eat some grouper tonight," Ted said. "It's my favorite fish."

I said it was mine, too.

We headed to a tiny Islamorada restaurant. As we walked in, Ted said to the hostess, "Oh, it's great to be here in Miami."

She chuckled at him and said, "Oh, Mr. Williams, you know this isn't Miami." She took us to our table, and Ted kidded and played word games with our waitress for the rest of the night.

We ate like kings, and later in the evening, Ted said, "You boys will spend the night."

"I'm sorry, we can't," I said. "We're chartering a boat at six in the morning."

"Well, just stay here and get up at four a.m.," he said.

We all laughed and finished our grouper and white wine. Ted picked up the check, and we said our goodbyes to end a dream of an evening.

I'll always remember that night, in part because of how Ted told us about how he loved hitting against my dad and how much he respected him. That sentiment is one I have found to be universal. If Dizzy Trout met someone or addressed a crowd, they remembered him. When he spoke, he demanded attention. He was special. He was larger than life. People wanted to be with him. He was, for lack of a better word, memorable.

He'd surprise you, too; keep you on your toes and change the flow of the river. He'd go out with the guys and bring five of them home for breakfast at two in the morning, and my mom would get up and cook for everyone. He was the kind of guy who would, out of nowhere, pull up in front of the house with five dump trucks full of gravel and announce to everyone that it was time to resurface the driveway.

He was a natural, both as a man and an athlete. He loved to play golf and could shoot in the 70s without practicing. Many times he'd send all us kids across the street and over the river that ran outside our house. We'd bring our gloves and helmets, and he'd hit a 7- or 8-iron; and as he'd hit balls, we'd catch them, and that's how he practiced. He could bowl a 200 game in his sleep.

The only thing that got the best of him was stomach cancer. He was only in his mid-50s when it started eating him up from the inside out, day by day. He dropped to less than 100 pounds near the end, and we couldn't do much except be with him and put hot, wet towels on his belly to help ease the pain.

I was in eighth grade when he died February 28, 1972. We got a phone call from the hospital that morning. We were home. I heard the whispers of his passing crawling through the house. They told me he was gone. The next day, without mom knowing, I put on his dark over-sized coat and his hat and snuck out to get a job at our local grocery store to provide for my family. A day later the manager called mom and said I couldn't work there because I was too young.

Thanks to White Sox, Bill Veeck and Leo Breen, monthly checks would continue to appear in our mailbox for years to come, kind of like dad, still taking care of his brood.

Aunt Ruth still has memories of that meeting at Briggs Stadium more than 60 years ago. From the meeting came a happy 33-year marriage, 10 beautiful children, lots of grandchildren, and even more great-grandchildren.

Ruth still shares all those memories with our family, and she remembers that her sister really did care.

	1	2	3	4	5	6	7	8	9	R	H	E
Visitor	0	0	0									
Home	1	0	2									

"The Souper"

As Trout boys kept coming and coming, all of our family and the Trout family's relatives and friends couldn't help wondering: Which one would be born with the Major League arm?

Each of the eight kids before me passed through childhood without showing any particular inclination toward the game. People were starting to wonder if maybe the Trout baseball gene hadn't been passed down. Of the seven boys and three girls in our family, none of the other boys played baseball, at least not regularly. My brother Ross was the most involved. He's now the head librarian at Andrew High School in Tinley Park, Illinois, and for a while he played ball for a junior college.

The big league arm was only passed down to the ninth child — me.

Some pro athletes say they had a "defining moment," a time when they were young and everyone just knew that they had what it took. Maybe they hit a ball over a faraway roof or threw it through a wooden fence — something so remarkable everyone knew they were the one.

For me, there wasn't one defining moment, there were two. My moments weren't quite so dramatic, but still, they were moments — and unforgettable in their own way.

The first time I was nine years old at a "Hit, Run and Throw" competition at a neighborhood park in South Holland. It reminds me of "Rookie of the Year," the movie where the kid breaks his arm, and when they repair it, he owns an arm so strong that he goes on to pitch for the Cubs. At this "Hit, Run and Throw," they had the boundaries marked off on the baseball field for what they thought a 13-year-old kid could throw, and the people watching lined up around the boundaries. I didn't hit it as far as the other kids in my category. The throwing, though, was something else. They had a spot marked for the farthest a kid could throw, and I threw the softball over everybody's head — over the end line and way over the crowd. Jaws dropped, and I won first place. Today, if that had happened, I'd probably have an agent come over to try and sign me up.

The second moment was unforgettable not so much for what I did, but for who saw me do it.

My father had a friend named Bill Campbell, who was a commercial painter. We were up at the Campbells' vacation home in Michigan the summer when I was 12 years old, and I had my glove with me, as most kids do at that age. I was playing catch with a guy, and pretty soon, the glove started popping. *Pop! Pop! Pop!* Louder and louder. I was stretching my arm out, and before I knew it, I looked behind me to see my dad standing there with his friends. He stood there for a while, just watching, and listening for that sweet sound of ball slamming into glove. Finally, it was like a light bulb flicked on in his head. He turned around all of a sudden and yelled out, "Somebody go get Pearl! This is the little SOB who can pitch! And tell her we can stop having kids, too!"

After that, everybody knew I had a "souper." That's what Major Leaguers called their arms for many years. Now, they say it's your "hose." The name "souper" comes from "soup bone" which is what old-timers called their throwing arms. Why? Because the arm on a man is the equivalent of the front leg on a beef cow which was usually used to make soup stock; therefore, soup bone. Older players would come up to you on the day you pitched and say, "How's the old souper today, Diz?"

Dad wouldn't be around to see me develop into one of the best high school pitchers in the country. So I'm glad he found out that summer at the Campbells' that I had been given the arm because it was only a couple of years later that he passed away.

As much as Dad's job revolved around baseball, we were never a baseball family. Luckily, we lived across from an open field, and I'd walk over there and start throwing long balls, pick up the ball, throw it long again, and repeat until I was tired. Throwing long is the best thing for your arm.

With a family as big as we had, I never played competitive baseball with a brother. For them, that was probably a good thing.

The brother who had the most influence on me was Richard. When I was five, he asked me to choke up on the bat. And I looked at him as if to say, "I'm not sick," thinking he wanted me to throw up on the bat. He explained what he meant.

My brother Bob is a chef and has nothing to do with baseball, other than he drinks Budweisers in the stands.

My oldest brother Paul was always putting us in precarious situations. He'd take us down to the basement and tie my arm to my brother Johnny's arm, and we would box. Once I happened to catch him with my left and knocked his front tooth out. All I did for the next two days was hide from Johnny. Paul would always have his two brothers downstairs and absolutely screaming. He'd give us the Chinese water torture. Or he would do things like stand on the second level of the house and throw money on the floor of the living room. Then he'd watch four or five of us fight for dimes and nickels. If quarters were involved, often blood would be, too. Paul is an English professor at Montana State now. He has no kids, probably because he saw all 10 of us grow up, and that was enough to make him vow never to have any.

My brother John was very quirky, very into science. One time he was putting sulfur and other chemicals into a test tube, and he chased me around the kitchen table with it until I hit him in the arm. The chemicals went up into his face, and his eyes burned for days. That incident is the reason why John has bad eyesight today. Also, he would climb up a 30-foot street light pole and hide his money in an electrical box so nobody could get it. We were a year and a half apart in age and constantly battling for friends. One day one of my friends told me John was going to make a cue ball that would explode when I hit it.

Another brother, Gary, was a great athlete in high school, but he got into drugs, heroin addiction. He's made his way through all that, and now he's clean and sober and helps others in need of counseling. When we were kids, we'd get into scraps every now and then. When I was 15, I saw him take some money off a card table we had, and I told him, "That's not fair!" He took a Coke bottle and broke it over my left elbow. Blood was everywhere. You can still see the blood stains on the card table and the scars on my elbow. Many thought that was the end of my pitching days, but after the glass was taken out by the doctor, he saw no severe damage to the elbow. My real baseball brother was Ross. We'd play Whiffle ball in the back yard, and we'd have lineup cards and base paths. We scuffed a bare spot in the grass so it looked like a mound, and my mom never really bothered us about that. Those Whiffle ball games taught me as much about learning spins and pitching control as anything else. Sometimes I'd play rubber-ball-fast-pitch with the guys down at a drugstore wall at Pacesetter Plaza in our neighbor-hood. The guys inside the store didn't appreciate it. The ball was only rubber, but I could throw so hard that the sound thundered through the store, and the manager often came out into the parking lot and asked us to stop.

Not having my dad around as a teenager made the years he and I did have together more precious. Even though Dad played and loved the game like one of his own children, he was anything but a Little League parent. Some kids can't stop shaking when they're on the field for fear their psychotic parents will yell something and embarrass the hell out of them. My dad was the exact opposite. When I was with the South Holland Trust and Savings team, I never knew when he was there. He was there more than I thought, I guess, but he would never sit in the stands or stand in a place where I could look over and see him from the pitching mound. He thought I would get too nervous.

One day when I was pitching I looked out of the corner of my eye and saw this funny-looking tree. It was Dad. He was standing behind the tree, not wanting to be noticed, except that his body was wider than the tree and he was sticking out. He made me nervous when he came to the games, but he also made me want to do better.

To me, what helped the most was my dad let me play without screaming and yelling. For a baseball dad, he was very reserved. In fact, one of the things he did when we played in the back yard was work with me on my hitting and defense. He thought a left-handed hitting first baseman who could hit was the fastest path to the Majors.

He also really knew how kids felt. He was very low-key in instructing me on the game, but when he did clinics, he would stress, "You've got to keep your ass down on the ground ball. That's the most important thing." I loved to see him demonstrate. Here was this big man who had an ample belly, showing little kids how to squat.

The best part was that even though I grew up with baseball in my life, being a Major Leaguer was never the ultimate goal. Making "The Show" was never mentioned. It just hung there, and everybody knew it was there for the taking when the time was right. That made baseball fun when I was a kid.

* * *

Because of Dad's job, we had a station wagon with the White Sox logo painted on both sides, and I always thought I was the coolest kid in town when I sat in Dad's car. That car made us official baseball power brokers.

Dad used to bring home Sox players like "No-Neck" Walt

Williams, who I saw years later as a coach with Texas; Tommy John, one of the great pitchers of his era; and Pete Ward, a first baseman-third baseman back then. Just being nine or 10 years old, I didn't know how cool that was because my dad himself was almost bigger than life. But my friends and their dads thought it was special.

When I was 11, a friend of mine invited me to a birthday party, and I remember shooting off my mouth about how all these famous baseball players were over at my house. It was no big deal to me. So the father of the birthday boy came over and said, "These guys are at your house, now?"

And I said, "Yeah. They're always at my house."

I decided that as a birthday present I would get my friend an autographed baseball with all these people on it, so I ran home. None of the guys was there that day, but I knew my dad was. And that was all I needed. One of his many talents was his penmanship. He'd been working for years as the public relations man for the White Sox, and many times he would sign the names of the players on the baseballs when they were too tired or too busy to do it. Dad's forgeries were amazing. He could write anybody's name exactly the way they wrote it. Carlos May, Dick Allen; he was perfect at it.

But this time, I ran home and told him, "Dad, I promised this kid I would get him a baseball with all these different players' names on it."

Dad signed 10 or 15 names, and I grabbed it and ran back to the party. I gave it to my friend, but my friend's dad took it from him and with his face excited as his 12-year-old's, said, "Wow, this guy's there, that guy's there? Hey, do you mind if we go over there and meet the players?"

And I said, "Well, I think they might just be on their way out." Fortunately for me, it worked. I thought for sure I would get caught, which would have meant no birthday cake for sure.

* * *

Looking back, having those players around helped me develop into a strong pitcher, because it gave me a "this-is-your-life" feeling. Being overwhelmed by the pros was not something that would happen to me. It's funny, but I seem to have matured early in some ways and late in others. As a kid and through high school, nothing seemed to bother me. I was just having fun playing the game.

I can remember a particular game in high school. It was pretty cold, like it usually is during the Illinois baseball season. The weather doesn't warm up until mid-April, and by then there are only a few weeks left. This particular game was early in my freshman year against our rival, Thornton Fractional North. I was warming up and throwing pretty hard, and their lead-off hitter saw this. I don't know if he was scared or what, but the umpire yelled, "Play Ball!" and the kid just stood there. He wasn't going up to the plate. The coach was yelling at him to get up there and bat. So I started throwing without a man in the batter's box. The count was strike two before the kid dared to step in there. I earned a very easy strikeout that way.

When I was on the mound, I was in control. I was 14 years old when I started throwing breaking balls, which I think is the proper age to start, and that was when people started seeing my ability. They always say that the ultimate pitcher would have an 18-year-old's arm and a 35-year-old's mind. This couldn't be more true. As a high schooler, I had all the pitches. But it would be many years before I would actually learn how to pitch.

Back then, I didn't care. It was just wind up and throw. I was just following the advice Dad would always tell me: "Don't think, son. Just throw the damn ball." Of all the lessons he taught me, this would be the hardest — as I would learn as a Major Leaguer.

All you kids out there who are pitchers remember this: The worst enemy you have isn't the opposing batters, your manager or the fan heckling you from the fourth row. Your own worst enemy is yourself. Thinking too much is a state of mind that comes not from others, but from our own nervous tendencies and fear of failure. When pitching on the sidelines, put yourself in game situations and feel the experience in your mind first. If you conquer your fears, you will conquer pitching.

Remember that throwing a baseball is a simple art. When you're young, you don't need breaking balls. Don't try to be tricky on the mound. Learn how to throw the ball far and straight and hard, and most importantly, like my dad always said, have fun. Be a good teammate, and try to get better each and every day. Even at the age of 18, when you think you know everything, you can pick up pointers about the finer points of pitching.

When I was starting my career with the White Sox, Milt May, our catcher at the time, tried to set me straight on what it would take. "No changeups until the third inning," he said. I was shocked. "What? What are you talking about? I make my living off of this," and I wiggled my four fingers, giving him the signal for the changeup.

And he said, "No changeups until we have to go to it. Why show them what you've got until you have to bring it out?"

And you know what? He was right. Milt or any good catcher will make the pitcher stay with his fastball and changeup until the other team starts to hit it, and then you mix it up a bit. If you've got stuff, you might never have to use it, and if you do run into turbulence, you need another pitch to unveil so you can keep them guessing. Your fastball has to create outs early in the game. If it doesn't, you're in trouble. Pitchers must learn two major elements: one is, throw strikes; the other is, work both sides of the plate.

Another mistake is to think, "Hey, I've got to get these guys out. It's up to me." That trap — thinking that you have to do more — is one pitchers fall into every day. If you just keep throwing that fastball, many hitters will play right into your hand. They'll try to pull an outside fastball and ground out, or they'll try to jack one out of the park with an uppercut swing and pop up a rising fastball on what should have been ball three. Always remember: Your fielders are behind you; use them; give the old souper a break.

In terms of approaching hitters, just remember the credo of the pitcher: high and inside, low and away. One of the greatest sports books ever is *Ball Four* by former Major Leaguer Jim Bouton. In that book, he wrote about how his managers and pitching coaches would approach him when he was playing. He would be struggling in the fourth inning, the coach would walk out of the dugout, all serious, and when he reached the top of the hill, he would say something like, "All right. Yastrzemski's coming up next. You want to give him the fastball high and tight, and the breaking stuff low and away." And Bouton would almost fall over laughing because that's how every pitcher tries to hand-cuff every hitter. If God were at the plate, you would take him high and tight, and low and away. God would be one tough out, but you get the idea. It's just common sense.

What also makes sense is not letting the best player on the other team beat you. During my career, there were a few guys who would hammer me every time I faced them, one being Dave Parker, the toughest hitter I ever faced. But heading into a game, I knew the guy who could transform a victory into an early shower with one swing. If you're pitching against the White Sox, don't let Frank Thomas beat you. If you're playing the Cubs, don't let

Sammy Sosa beat you. When I first came up in the American League, Reggie Jackson would beat you in a pressure situation. He was great at that. I think of St. Louis with Andy Van Slyke. He could beat you too, and he could go the other way with a pitch that wasn't even a mistake. Every team had one guy you watched for, such as Dave Winfield, when he was with the Padres, and Bobby Grich who was the Angels dangerous hitter. These are the players you must beware. One time, a team walked Ted Williams with the bases loaded because they figured he'd do less damage that way than if they'd let him put wood on the ball.

Here's a question: Would you rather face a .250-hitter who's four-for-four or a .320-hitter who's zero-for-8? I'll take my chances with the .250-hitter. His odds of reaching on a hit are still one-in-four in my mind because he's got the skills of a .250-hitter. The .320-hitter has more tools, quicker hands and wrists, and a more level swing which allows him a better chance to put the ball in play.

You have to look at who can swing the bat, then play the percentages. No, it's not easy. That little voice in the back of your mind, your ego, is always whispering, "Come on, man. You've got the stuff. Blow this guy away. You can get him out." The smart pitchers don't listen or, if they're lucky, have managers who take the decision out of their hands. Sometimes you need that manager as a third party who's not attached to the situation as much as you are.

During my career, we held pre-game meetings all the time, and I'd usually try to avoid them. I didn't want to get into all the strategies and trying to figure out each hitter. If you're going to go down the list of hitters, one through nine, you're going to become absorbed in their tendencies instead of what you need to do. It's too much, and a lot of it is unneeded. "Don't think, son. Just throw the damn ball." Dad knew what he was talking about.

If you're throwing strikes, high and inside, and low and away, the 1927 Yankees could be up there and you're going to get most of them out. Good pitching gets good hitting out most of the time. It's when you make mistakes on the mound or you walk hitters that you lose the ball game. But if you're throwing with velocity and movement, it doesn't matter who's up at the plate.

The right way to pitch is to throw strikes and *let* them hit the ball. That cuts down your pitch count. Throwing strikes is the most direct route to success. It's amazing how a 2-0 count makes a .180 hitter a .290 hitter. Too often during my career I fell behind in the count. I felt like every time I took the mound I had to have great stuff, I had to paint the corners and win the game. More often than not, I ended up in trouble. Harder is not always better. My troubles started when I tried to strike guys out instead of throwing my sinker to induce them to hit grounders.

Back as a high schooler, of course, none of this made sense to me. I had never had that seed planted in my head that "hitters get themselves out." No, in my mind it was the responsibility of a good pitcher like myself to overpower them and make sure they didn't hit the ball. My job was to throw the ball fast and leave nothing to chance. I was growing up as a typical kid having a great childhood and remaining oblivious to what was swirling around me. Even as late as my senior year in high school, I was naïve. I asked my coach, Don McAlvey, "Who are these 35 scouts here to see?" And he said, "You, you dummy."

What did I know? I was just a kid playing a game. It was so normal for me to play baseball that I didn't really feel I stood out. I was just a kid who loved to play baseball, and when I wasn't playing baseball, I loved to run around Comiskey Park while my dad was at work.

During the season, my dad would let us onto the field to hang out with the players before the game. My first experience with tobacco came at Comiskey Park when the White Sox manager back in the late 1960s, Eddie Stanky, gave me a wad of chew. Fifteen minutes later, I was headed for the dugout, green, sick and throwing up. They got a kick out of that one.

And when the Sox were out of town or during the off-season, my brother and I would skateboard up and down the ramps at the park. We would lock the restroom stall doors from the inside, then climb out and wait for our victim, usually a high-ranking Sox executive, to show up. Inevitably, we'd hear that cry for help from a front office executive, "Damn it, Dizzy, your kids locked the damn stall doors again."

That stunt was a staple of our good times at Old Comiskey. We would invade the clubhouse and pretend there was a game going on. We would get the baseball dispenser. Remember the "umpire-favor" basket that popped up out of the ground from behind home plate? I loved to watch the umpires take balls out of the basket. Sometimes Dad would sit in the hot tub in the clubhouse while we tore around the place.

Another time, in 1970, Dad brought me to Comiskey and introduced me to Tommy John. Because we were both lefties, Tommy gave me his glove, and for the next week, I couldn't stop looking at it. A White Sox player, Tommy John no less, had presented me with his very own glove.

Tommy John had his own little quirks. He used to bring his own shower heads on road trips to places like Cleveland and Detroit which had the smallest and grubbiest locker rooms. He would replace their shower heads with his own while we were in town, then take them back when we left. I found that very bizarre for him to walk on the team bus as we headed out to the airport with a bag full of shower heads. I guess he just wanted everyone to smell good.

I had no way of knowing it then, but 17 years later Tommy and I would be teammates on the New York Yankees.

	1	2	3	4	5	6	7	8	9	R	H	E
Visitor	0	0	0	1								
Home	1	0	2	1								

South Sider

Many seniors in high school have an idea what they want to do when they grow up. I did. I wanted to study forestry and become a park ranger. It was my idea of a wonderful lifestyle: no pressures, laid-back, becoming one with nature.

Instead, baseball stuck out its hand and offered me a ride. I was not ready. Without Dad around to force me down the straight path, I was a teenager happy to let the waves toss me wherever they wanted.

In South Holland, we lived next to a very rambunctious Irish family, and one of the sons was naturally named Pat. You could meet guys in bars for 50 years and never meet another guy like him. He had an influence on me that was good and bad. He was a catcher in high school and always gave me a high dose of confidence whenever he caught me. But he was also a partier. He was my biggest supporter, but he was never without a beer or a joint. He was actually best man at my wedding in '78, but later he would become an influence on me that would have a negative impact on me and our marriage. The road seems to lead to alcohol for many professional athletes, and friends like Pat sometimes help grease the way.

My senior year hadn't made me much older or wiser when graduation day at Thornwood came. It was the same day as the Major League Baseball draft, but the mountain air in Montana was too much of a draw. So instead of waiting at my house to see who'd select me, I visited my brother and did a little on-site research in Bozeman, Montana, home of Montana State University. We scaled Mount Baldy, camped overnight, then turned around and went back down the next day. When we reached the bottom, I found out there was another mountain for me to climb. A piece of yellow notepad paper fluttered on my brother's door. "Call home," it said. "You've been drafted by the White Sox." Steve Trout, forest ranger, was about to become Steve Trout, pro baseball player.

The Sox had the sixth pick in the Draft, and they picked me. I was going to play for Bill Veeck, my father's very good friend.

That winter Mr. Veeck gave me my second job as a phone solicitor, renewing contracts with season ticket holders.

Mr. Veeck was up to his old tricks again. Actually, this story falls into the Eddie Gaedel mode. The press and I were all in the board room at old Comiskey Park when the Sox announced the signing of Harry Chappas, a diminutive shortstop. They had Harry stand next to a great big check, like those kind you see being given to pro golfers when they win a tournament. A banner behind him read: "The biggest check to the smallest player for the smallest amount." Harry Chappas stood a mere 5'3" and weighed all of 150 pounds. Mr. Veeck realized that Harry was a possible drawing card because Harry was Greek and Chicago had a quarter of a million Greek-Americans.

This publicity stunt reminds me of the 1951 Eddie Gaedel story when Mr. Veeck owned the St. Louis Browns. Eddie stood all of 3'7" and weighed 65 pounds. A trailer carrying a *papier-mâché* cake was rolled onto the field between games of a double-header against the Detroit Tigers. Out jumped Eddie wearing a Browns uniform with the number "1/8" on the back. No one knew at the time that Eddie would be sent up to pinch-hit. Detroit pitcher Bob Cain and his catcher Bob Swift consulted on the mound. Cain asked if he should pitch underhand to him, and Swift told him to pitch to him like any other hitter. Gaedel had a strike zone about as big as a baby's bib, so Cain walked him on four pitches. A pinch-runner was put in for him, and he ran into the dugout to the roars and applause of the appreciative fans. That was the extent of Eddie's big league career.

My dad, who was still with the Tigers that year, later told Cain, if he'd been pitching, he would have plunked Gaedel right between the eyes. Cain said he wished he could be remembered for some of the other things he did in baseball instead of just throwing four balls to a little person. Quite unfortunately, Gaedel's life came to a sudden halt in 1961 at the age of 36 when he died from injuries suffered in a mugging. Cain and his wife attended little Eddie's funeral in Chicago.

Bill Veeck was a pure baseball owner and fan. He knew how to sell the game and make it entertaining as well as competitive. He was jovial guy who liked a good time as much as anybody.

One night he and friends were at a party, and around two in

the morning, he asked for another beer. The host informed him that he was out of beer, to which Mr. Veeck promptly replied: "If you're out of beer, you're out of Bill." Mr. Veeck and friends left and went to one of his favorite watering holes, Miller's Pub on Wabash and Adams in Chicago.

In 1959, Mr. Veeck unveiled uniforms with the players' names on the back. He and his wife Mary Frances were watching a game on television when Bill noticed that the TV viewers got all the information about they players: name, position, other statistics. He wanted the customer in the ballpark to have the same information.

I believe Mr. Veeck would never do some of today's gimmicks like "the Noise Meter," or stupid games on the screen. Today, nobody can just sit and discuss the beauty of the game. It's all about loud noise and sponsors making sure the fans know about the latest Ameritech promotion.

Mr. Veeck upset the radio networks in 1948 when his Cleveland Indians played in the World Series. They told him he couldn't have his own announcers do the games. The networks were going to replace them, but Bill said no way. He felt the announcers were there all year and they helped the team. They should keep on announcing right through the World Series. The station gave in.

One day while I was running on Waveland Avenue after batting practice, I noticed a guy crossing the street with a slight defect in his step. As I got closer, I realized it was Bill Veeck all by himself. We stopped and talked. He was heading to Wrigley Field to buy a ticket in the bleachers where he could sit and have a beer with his shirt off and enjoy a Cub game.

That was Mr. Veeck's natural element: the outfield bleachers with the fans. He loved it there. Little did people know that he was really very accessible. All anybody had to do was look up his number in the public telephone book and give him a call.

I'm really so proud that Mr. Veeck had such a close family relationship with my dad and he gave me a shot to play for him. He passed away in 1986, leaving a gaping hole in baseball that may never be filled again.

* * *

Throughout high school, I had avoided thinking about the scouts, the pressure, and the expectations of pro ball. I just wanted to be a kid. But as soon as I scribbled my name on the bottom of that Major League contract, though, it was time to grow up. I was off to rookie ball in Sarasota, Florida, the first time I had been away from home on my own.

A man named Sam Hairston met me at the airport. He was the father of Jerry Hairston of the White Sox, one of the best pinch-hitters in the American League. Jerry's son, Jerry Jr., is now a rising star as a second baseman with the Orioles. Being a rookie scared me frantic, and it was Sam's job to show me the ropes and make me feel at home, which wasn't easy. He took me to my first home-away-from-home.

The Sox Motor Hotel, which the White Sox owned, was a strange place to me. It had a pool, shuffleboard, and a laundry service. You knew this was a different kind of place, everybody in the same surroundings, right next to the workout complex in Sarasota. On my first night down there, I shut myself in my room because I was lonely and afraid. That first morning seemed as if it would never come, and I bounced off the walls. Even now, I can remember clenching my hand into a fist and slamming it into the flimsy wall of the hotel more than a few times. If I managed to break my hand, I figured, I could go back home and be with my family again. I don't remember falling asleep. Much to my amazement, the sun did come up the next morning, and with it came my first workout as a professional baseball player.

My first pro contract called for a $35,000 bonus, so I bought a new Monte Carlo to cruise town. But my stay in Sarasota and rookie ball was short. Soon, it was on to instructional league, where you really get your first taste of professional baseball. Instructional league is where they send the cream of the crop, the future Major Leaguers.

The Sox had optioned me to Boston, which meant I would play instructional ball for the Red Sox, while still remaining property of the White Sox. This formality did not protect me from being the butt of some practical jokes.

One day on the way home on the team bus after a game against the Pirates, the Boston guys reeled me in on one of the standard baseball gags of the ages. A couple of the guys said, "Hey, man, Timmy can pick three people up off the ground."

I sat there, and I thought. Then I said, "There's no way he can pick up three guys. He's not that strong."

They came right back at me, "Steve, you don't think he can? Why don't you be one of the three guys?"

At this point, I figured, he's not going to be able to pick up three guys. They had two of the biggest guys lie down on the floor, and I was in the middle. We interlocked arms and legs, so that we bonded together, ready to be lifted up. Of course, the guy in the middle is at the mercy of the other two, and it was then I realized I was in trouble. Seconds later, everybody on the team got coffee, hot soup, shaving cream, chewing tobacco, toilet water — whatever they wanted — and dumped it all over me.

I couldn't believe it. I was humiliated, I yelled, I tried to fight back, but I couldn't do anything. The next day, I didn't want to be around anybody. I hated everyone. Finally, "Broadway" Charlie Wagner came up to me and said, "Steve, they only do this to the guys they think are going to make the big leagues." That put a different spin on it altogether, and as it turned out, Charlie was right. He was someone I really liked and respected. He had a short career in the Majors, six years, all with the Boston Red Sox. He became a regular starter in 1941 and won 12 games while losing eight. The next year he had 14 wins against 11 losses before he was called off to the war. He came back briefly in 1946, but that was the end of his Major League career. Overall, he won 32 and lost 23 with a very respectable ERA of 3.91. People said he earned his nickname because when he pitched in the big leagues for the Red Sox in the 1940s, he was a sharp dresser. I still see him at times, and he's the same as he ever was: classy, mature, and dignified.

In 1977, I started in Class A ball in Wisconsin with the Appleton Foxes. Appleton, hometown of Harry Houdini, was a wonderful experience for me. It was a real baseball town, and the Foxes manager was a guy named Gordie Lund.

Many players stayed in family homes, and one guy's house even had a pool table and a keg. As you might guess, we hung out there a lot. I stayed in a cabin about 20 miles out of town by myself, which I enjoyed; but I also had one of the longest commutes to practices and games. One time I missed the team bus when we were leaving for a trip to Davenport, Iowa. I showed up at the parking lot, and they said I should just drive to Davenport myself. When I got there, Gordie was waiting, and as we greeted each other, he put out his hand, took the keys to my car, and kept them. I guess he didn't trust me — and with good reason. But I had an extra set of keys. After the game, a bunch of guys and I headed to the Pizza Hut for some food and beer. When we got back to the hotel, Gordie was waiting in the lot in his pajamas. He took the second set of keys, too. He also tried to show me who was boss. He grabbed my hair and started pulling it. I pushed him away. I felt violated. From then on, I thought of him negatively. This was the start of my negative feelings for some people I was working for in baseball.

I didn't stay long in Appleton. I was 6-6 with a 4.10 ERA halfway through the season. That included a span where I gave up just five runs in 23 innings and won three straight. The Sox promoted me to Triple-A in Des Moines, Iowa. My manager there was a guy named Joe Sparks, a great leader and a great guy, one of the managers I truly liked. He was a big, strong fellow who just had a way about him — respected and hardworking.

Triple-A was much more intense than Class A. Today, the best prospects play in Double-A, and Triple-A is for the veterans and owners who are in the business of minor league baseball. The players are guys 27-30 with little chance of seeing the big leagues again. Double-A has the cream of the crop, and it's less competitive and more hopeful. In those days, though, Triple-A was the stepping stone to the Majors. The pay was a lot better, too. I was making about $550 a month in Appleton, and in Des Moines, with the Iowa Oaks, that shot up to $900. Some guys would steal soup from the clubhouse just to make ends meet. I cashed in on the remarkable pool talents I had honed as a youth and made some extra money at the local pool halls.

But life was good, and in no small part because my girlfriend, Sandy Belder, had decided to move with me to Des Moines. We had first met in 1974, when I was 17. I fell in love with her the first time I saw her, a chance meeting. One of the other girls in the neighborhood would ask me out all the time, and after so much of that, I finally said yes. We decided to attend a party at the house of a guy who lived in the neighborhood, and when I walked into the basement, a girl was leaning against this pole, as if God had put her there just to wait for me. I walked up to her and said, "Would you like to get some air?" She said yes, and when we went outside, I couldn't stop looking at her. I finally found the nerve to tell her, "You are the prettiest girl I've ever seen." We talked some more, and later, I persuaded her to give me her phone number. I wrote it on the hood of my friend's car with a pencil eraser, and to this day, I remember the number. As soon as I got home, I wrote it out in big magic marker.

I called her the next day. The day after that, too. Sandy ducked me every time I called, but I wouldn't be denied. Her brother Don was the equipment guy on the Thornwood High basketball team, and I remember telling a friend of his that if he had any influence in getting us married, I'd buy him a pink Cadillac. But progress was slow. So I tried to take out Sandy's sister, and I think that's when Sandy grew jealous and decided to give me a shot.

When I went to the Instructional League in 1976, Sandy was in school at Eastern Illinois University and I wrote her a letter every day. I came home from the Instructional League in late October, and we dated during the off-season. I remember that time well because my two favorite groups were "The Average White Band" and "Earth, Wind and Fire," and I made sure I'd have it on in the background anytime I called Sandy. The next year I went to the Appleton Foxes, the A-ball affiliate of the White Sox, but I still kept after her. I would pitch a game in Appleton, then drive four hours to see her. Eventually, she realized I wasn't going to give up.

When Triple-A called, I begged her to come with me, and she did. We had an apartment together in Des Moines and finished the season there. That off-season — February 4, 1978 — we were married.

A few months later the Sox sent me to Double-A Knoxville, where the manager was Tony LaRussa, a young up-and-comer just learning the ropes in the White Sox farm system. Everything began coming together in Knoxville. Sandy was there with me. I started a game every four or five days. The first three months of the '78 season, I went 8-3 with a 1.56 ERA, but I was making only $1,000 a month.

One day we were in a mall in Knoxville, and Sandy came out of a card shop, crying. "I wanted to buy something special for my dad for his birthday, but I couldn't afford it," she said. I went immediately to a phone and called C.V. Davis, the minor league director for the White Sox, to explain our trouble. "C.V.," I said, "can I get a little more money?" I filled him in on the situation, about how Sandy wanted to buy the card but couldn't. C.V. said, "How about if I send you to back to A-ball in Appleton, where the cost of living is cheaper?" That's when I realized that this game is strictly business.

Our financial situation would change on June 29, when the unexpected happened. The team was in Birmingham at a movie theater, killing time after a rainout by watching the movie "F.I.S.T." with Sylvester Stallone. Right in the middle of the movie, as we're all stretched out, LaRussa taps me on the shoulder and says, "Can you pitch tomorrow?"

I had just pitched a couple of days earlier, but I said, "Yeah, but it's not my turn to pitch."

LaRussa said, "No, I mean can you pitch in Minneapolis for the big league club."

I said, "Damn! You bet I can!"

I yelled, and my teammates and I ditched the movie in the middle and went out for beer and pizza.

The next day LaRussa drove me to the airport at five in the morning on the team bus. That was the easiest part of going to Minnesota to meet the White Sox. Many hours passed. My connecting flight in Texas didn't connect. Eventually, I arrived in Minneapolis, but my bags didn't. I walked up to the gate at Metropolitan Stadium without credentials. I was a 20-year-old kid with long hair, dressed in Double-A attire, by myself, with a big bag of carry-on goods and no uniform — it was on the other flight. I said, "I'm Steve Trout. The White Sox just called me up, and I'm pitching today."

The security guard said, "Sure, you just got called up. And I own the Twins."

Someone from the clubhouse finally came to the gate and vouched for me. I remember tip-toeing into the clubhouse at the old Met and seeing all these Major League players there and all this ice cream, soda pop, and cookies on the table in the corner. Sitting around the place were players like Ralph Garr, the speedy outfielder they nicknamed "Roadrunner," and knuckleballing pitcher Wilbur Wood, who would sit at his locker and tie flies for fishing. This was not a Double-A locker room, for sure.

No Double-A hitters came up to the plate, either, when I finally did take the mound. They had put me in to mop up the late innings of a 9-1 loss. Still, I think every pitcher remembers his first batter, the same way he never forgets his first love. My first batter was Butch Wynegar, who retired in 1988 and later coached for Texas. The adrenaline was pumping, and I struck him out on high-and-away fastballs that were coming in about 95 m.p.h. Our third baseman, Eric Soderholm, said I should keep the ball, so I did. In my one inning, I gave up a run. Rod Carew, the game's best hitter back then, was on base when I made the last guy pop up to end the inning.

After the game, a Chicago TV station put me on for a live interview, and people called in to ask questions. My brother Rich, a Chicago public school teacher for over 30 years, called in, and they put him on the air. I couldn't believe it, but I was happy to hear his voice. On the air, he asked me, "Hey, brother, what was it like facing Rod Carew?"

I said, "Hey, for $112 a day, I'd face him or anybody else." That was the minimum salary back then — 112 bucks a day. That's meal money these days.

That was my first big league experience.

After that game, I sat on the bench for four or five days, and then went back down to Triple -A in Des Moines. They called me up again for the last month of the season in 1978, and I won my first three decisions in the big leagues, one of them a shutout.

In my first win, I went six and a third innings, allowed five hits, walked one, and struck out four. However, it wasn't great pitching that got me my first big league win. I owe it all to "Disco Danny" Ford. The game was in the sixth inning, and I was in a little trouble with Ford on second, Jerry Morales on third, and two outs. The next hitter knocked one into the right field gap. Morales went half way so he could tag up if the ball was caught; however, "Disco Danny" made up his own mind that the ball would land safely. When he reached third, he turned around to watch the ball fall in for a hit. His back was actually toward home plate. Morales was still hesitating. I was trying to back up the play, and I saw Ford back-pedaling toward home plate and Morales still holding up but moving slowly toward third to be extra careful. But everybody was still watching the play in right-center field. Ford passed Morales in the basepath. I couldn't believe my own eyes. The umpire threw up both arms, called Ford out, which made the third out of the inning. The next day in the paper: DISCO DAN FORD FINED $5,000.

But that finish wasn't enough to earn me a spot on the big team for the start of the '79 season. They put me in Des Moines again, and I went 3-1 before I was called back to the big team on May 5, a Saturday. But this time I wasn't going to Minnesota, and I wouldn't be a reliever. Instead, I was heading to Detroit to start for the Sox, to pitch, toe the dirt, and sweat on the same mound where my father had 37 years earlier. Upon receiving the news, I called my mom and told her what was happening, that I would be starting two days later, and asked her to be there.

She said no at first. She hadn't gone to all of Dad's games when he pitched. She knew he became nervous when she was in the stands, and so did she. But I talked her into coming anyhow. The way she figured, it might be the only time she could see me pitch there. She rearranged her schedule at the apparel store where she worked and brought my sisters Laura and Connie, Laura's infant son Brian, and my wife Sandy to Detroit. As soon as Mom saw me taking my first warmup pitches, she started to cry. She hadn't been in Tiger Stadium since May, 1952, before the Tigers traded Dad to Boston.

Nervous as I was, I didn't pitch badly. I went into the eighth inning with a 4-3 lead, but then I hit Rusty Staub with a pitch. Steve Kemp then blooped a single to left. Because we didn't have a left-hander in the bullpen, our shortstop-manager at the time, Don Kessinger, let me pitch to Jason Thompson, a left-hander. Thompson botched a sacrifice bunt, then ended up singling in a run. Kessinger brought in a reliever named Mike Proly, and he gave up the game-winning single to Lance Parrish. That was it, a 5-4 loss.

After the game, all the papers and TV stations wanted to know what it was like to start a game at the same park where my dad had seen his finest days. I knew what it was like. I told them it was the most important feeling a person can have, to pitch on the same mound your father once pitched on. To know that 30 years earlier he was sweaty, bearing down on the hitter the same way I would do, in the same park, same dugouts, it was special. Unforgettable.

So was the rest of that 1979 season with the White Sox, some of the most magical times I had in baseball.

* * *

Old Comiskey Park was charming, like home to me. After all, it was the place I'd used as a playground from the time I was seven years old.

As a fan, Comiskey was a great place to see baseball, unless you were sitting behind a post. Otherwise, it was some ballpark. The scoreboard was unlike any other in baseball. Every time there was a home run, fireworks would shoot out the top — another baseball first from the brilliant marketing mind of Bill Veeck. You could feel the history of the park vibrating through it every day. The walk down from the clubhouse to the field was damp and unforgettable. Cleat marks had chewed away the wood on the floor of the tunnel, and chipped green paint — the park's trademark color — was everywhere. The light bulbs leading down the tunnel to the dugout were quirky and unpredictable, in part because sometimes a frustrated player would take the walk to the showers and bust a few bulbs on the way. Something about old Comiskey was completely compelling.

The best part of playing for the Sox was when we ran from foul line to foul line during pre-game workouts. The picnic area was located underneath the left field bleachers. Dad, who was in charge of community relations, was proud of that area. He loved to barbecue, and he wanted people to eat well when they were at the ballpark. That they did. The ladies started cooking the chicken in that picnic area, and the aroma of the food hovered over the outfield grass as you ran your sprints. As the fans filed in, the sky was often clear and beautiful, and you knew it was going to be a great night for baseball.

The only downer about Comiskey Park was the fans who did all the boozing. Sometimes when I'd be sitting in the dugout in the eighth inning with a good game going, I'd look up into the upper bleachers and see half of the right field upper deck and lower deck fighting it out. It was a bar, an outdoor saloon. I'd just sit there in this "Baseball Palace," as it was called when it was built, and ask myself, "Why do they have to fight?"

The new park isn't nearly the same as the old one. It's a huge pile of cement with very little baseball charm. It's very poorly situated. If they had built it so fans could see the beautiful lights of downtown Chicago during night games and the skyline during day games, then the new park would have something resembling character. They didn't build it that way because to situate it with the open side toward downtown would have been an inconvenience for *the stockholders*. Their parking area would have to be moved to an area that was considered dangerous, and they all opposed that.

One of the most famous nights at Old Comiskey was one of its most infamous: the Disco Demolition on July 12, 1979. The central figures in the whole operation were Mike Veeck, son of the White Sox owner, and Steve Dahl, back then an irreverent morning dee-jay at "The Loop," a rock station in Chicago. Dahl had made a career out of trashing disco music. He hated it in the way dogs hate fleas. Veeck, like his father, was the consummate marketing man. A few years ago he was a driving force behind the Northern League, a league based in Minnesota that packed in fans despite not having any affiliation with the Majors. Anyway, back in '79, Mike saw the potential of blending the Sox's "South Side Hit Men" image with the "Disco Sucks" crowd — at least for one night.

The idea was a promotion where fans could get in for 98 cents ("The Loop's" frequency) if they brought a disco record to the park. Between games of the twinbill against the Tigers, Dahl and some explosives would create a vinyl Armageddon in the middle of the outfield. 50,000 long-haired kids in black T-shirts were inside the park, and 50,000 more were outside, wanting to get in.

If anyone needed a clue that something very odd and dangerous was going to happen, they received it when the beer ran out in the fifth inning of the first game. A revved-up crowd of long-haired young people needed no other reason to go off the deep end.

From my perspective in the bullpen, though, it appeared to be a normal doubleheader. In between games, I was doing an interview with Harry Caray, and while we were standing there, Dahl walked by with a buxom blonde on each arm. The ladies were dressed in army fatigues. Harry gave them a good looking over and said, "Hey, Steve! What do you think about those two!"

And I said, "Hey, Harry, they're really good-looking."

Harry cut the interview short with me and started to interview Dahl and the girls, while throughout the park, fans wanted another beer as they waited to see the albums blown sky-high.

Dahl then set off the boom — and plenty more than that. Records went flying into the air. About 10,000 burned out teenagers in black T-shirts came tumbling out of the stands onto the field to trash the place. It was mayhem. Fans were everywhere. Smoke was everywhere. Shattered pieces of disco were everywhere. The mounted police rode onto the field to contain the mob, and the players headed for cover.

You would never think a smashed vinyl record could be a lethal weapon, but it is. Somebody whipped one from the outfield stands, and it stuck in the outfield grass like a javelin. As I walked off the field, another one almost speared me in the back. As I looked down at the album, all I could think was, "Shit, I could have been killed by the 'Village People!' All hell had broken loose. Lamar Johnson, our power-hitting first baseman, sat in the dugout with Ralph Garr and me. All of a sudden Lamar looked at me and asked, "Hey, Steve, these are all your friends, aren't they?" He was kidding.

Yet sure enough, right after Lamar said that, people started running in front of the dugout and saying, "Hey, Steve! We'll see you back home! We'll see you tomorrow!" It was all my crazy buddies from South Holland, right on cue.

Lamar and Ralph grabbed a couple of bats, and I said, "What are you going to do with those?"

They said, "If anybody comes down here, they're going to get hit!"

I said, "You can't do that. These are my friends!"

Finally, the police told us it might be a good idea to retreat to the clubhouse. Thousands of disco-haters were on the field, running around yelling and tearing up the grass. The cops tried to bring the scene under control, but the field was all torn up. The players felt trapped as they locked the doors to the clubhouse. About two hours later, they called the game, possibly the only one ever to be forfeited because of a backfired promotion. The other, I believe, was Cleveland with its 10-cent beer night. Some people say that was the day disco music died. I believe it hurt the image of disco music, but those people at the game hated disco anyway. So maybe some people got caught up in the demolition promotion, but disco continued and so did Steve Dahl.

So ended one of the watershed moments in Comiskey Park history, and it couldn't have happened to a team with an odder assortment of characters. The White Sox of the late 1970s and early '80s were a perfect fit for the way Mr. Veeck ran his ball club. They were affordable and entertaining, and right in the center ring of the circus were the two announcers, Harry Caray and Jimmy Piersall.

Everyone knows Harry as the former Cubs broadcaster on the superstation WGN. Before he went to the Cubs, though, he and Piersall were the most eccentric twosome in baseball. They broadcast the Sox games on WSNS, Channel 44, which wasn't even a network affiliate, but a UHF channel. If you didn't have a good antenna on your TV, you were out of luck.

Caray and Piersall fit in exactly with what Veeck wanted, which was entertainment, pure and simple. As you might guess, Harry had a reputation as a guy who would tip a beer or two during the broadcasts. Some game days, you could find Harry throwing down 7-and-7s and straight gin at a little Italian restaurant in some town on the road. At noon.

That was the broadcast team. Caray would ham it up. Piersall, the colorful whacko, would spend the whole game criticizing guys for how they couldn't field or how their fundamentals stunk and how he would have made the play. These guys were anything but "homers." If you played well, they praised you to no end. If you played poorly, they ripped you — hard.

People laughed at them and enjoyed them, but as a player you couldn't be fooled. These guys were powerful — to the point where they could make or break you, if not with the front office, then at least with the fans.

Once when we were on the road, I was pitching and really struggling. Harry apparently thought my focus wasn't what it should have been, so in the middle of the broadcast he says,

"Look at Trout! Somebody should go out there and slap the guy!" When we returned to Chicago, I'd go out for a beer, and all these guys remembered what Harry said during the game. My brother Gary made up a T-shirt that read, "Bury Harry." I was going to buy 10,000 of them and hand them out at the game.

Harry would pull crap like that all the time. I could never be good enough for him, and he had a special theme he hammered on: that I never had reached the potential he thought I had. It's a tough situation to be in. You're out there, sweating and working and trying to do your best, and in the meantime, these guys who think they are so knowledgeable about the game are ripping you in front of millions.

Harry knew people liked to hear the negative, and he often fulfilled that. One game Lamar Johnson took three pitches in a row — didn't even swing the bat. He ran into the clubhouse so he could listen to the radio to hear what Harry and Jimmy were saying about him. The week after that, LaRussa said, "No more radios or TVs in the clubhouse during the game." Even the clubhouse guy couldn't listen to it because guys kept running back in there to hear what Piersall and Caray were saying about them.

That was the power they had. The only consolation was to consider the source, especially when it was Piersall. Jimmy had an angry streak, something bitter. To this day, he's a friend, but I don't know why he's so bitter. His mouth is his worst enemy, for sure. You love his honesty, but sometimes, he's way over-board. "Political correctness" is not in Jimmy's vocabulary. He sees himself as an entertainer, so maybe that's the answer.

If you've ever heard Piersall on the radio or TV, you know that to say he's eccentric is an understatement. He played outfield for the Red Sox in the 1950s, then the Indians, Senators, Mets, and Angels in the '60s, and he was a .272 lifetime hitter. He might best be known for the story of his life, first as a book, then as a movie called "Fear Strikes Out" with Karl Malden as Piersall's dad and Anthony Perkins as Piersall. The movie, based on the book, chronicles the way Piersall's dad drove his son crazy with the constant pressure he placed on Jimmy to be a ballplayer. In one scene, Perkins climbs the fence behind home plate after scoring a run, screaming and scanning the crowd trying to find his father for approval. To this day, Piersall's catch phrase is, "I'm crazy, and I've got the papers to prove it."

During his playing career, he underwent counseling because he was so intense and off-center that he was eventually committed.

Legend has it that one time in a game at Yankee Stadium, he ran deep into center field and hid behind one of the statues that used to be on the playing field, and he wouldn't come out.

One time he was quoted as saying, "All the baseball wives are horny broads." It was all over the Chicago TV and radio stations, and at 8:15 the next morning I got a call from Wally Phillips, the big morning radio personality on WGN at the time. He woke me up and said, "Did you hear the latest comment from Piersall?"

I said, "Who? Piersall said it? So what? Look at the source!"

This was a guy who once right to my face said, "Trout, you're a bum." The first time I heard him say that, I thought, "Why did he say that? What did I do?" You just have to give it right back to him. That's just the way he is. One time at Milwaukee County Stadium I was in the hot tub relaxing. They had a little one-man tub. Piersall came in and stopped dead in his tracks. He barked out, "Twenty-one years old! Twenty-one years old! And you're in the hot tub!" He did that kind of thing to players all the time, and many of them hated him for it. The odd part of it all was that he was also one of the team's coaches. He would be up in the booth ripping you during a night game, and the very next day he'd be coaching you on the field before the game. Players had little respect for him in those dual roles.

Harry Caray died in February of 1998 out in Arizona. On the way to Harry's funeral, Jack Brickhouse, the man that Harry had succeeded in the telecaster's booth, had a medical emergency and had to go to the hospital. Six months later Jack died.

Not long after that came an announcement that a statue would be dedicated to Harry on Opening Day '99. Pretty soon Jack's widow, Pat, started receiving all sorts of calls from the local sports media who ask her to go on the air to tell the fans what the Cubs were planning to do to honor Jack on Opening Day. She told them, "I don't know why you're calling me. I don't know a thing about what the Cubs are doing for Jack." This went on all winter.

Finally, in spring training of '99, Pat was attending one of the fund-raising parties with the Cubs brass when John McDonough, vice-president of marketing and broadcasting with the Cubs, told her, "Pat, hang loose. We have something planned for Jack during the summer. I'll get back to you when we have a date." Pat was okay with that.

But when she returned to Chicago from spring training, Pat started getting more calls again from the media, and this time she went on the air to tell them she still didn't know. By the third show she was on, the fans got into the story, and everybody was asking what the Cubs were planning to do for Jack.

The Thursday before Opening Day McDonough called Pat and said, "I hope you're available for Opening Day." She told him she had a dental appointment that day. "We really want you there," said McDonough. She asked why, and he said, "Well, we're going to do something for Jack." When she asked what, he said, "It's a surprise." Pat believed, that, even at this time, less than a week before Opening Day, the Cubs had no idea what they would do to honor Jack, but she canceled the dental appointment and went to Wrigley for Opening Day.

She was in the dugout with Governor George Ryan and Walter Payton, which was his last public appearance before revealing his fatal illness. Pat was asked to speak, and she agreed to do it. She spoke eloquently. While standing next to Hall of Famers Ernie Banks and Billy Williams, she saw "Hey Hey" on the foul poles for the very first time.

Later the media wanted to talk to her, and by the fifth inning, the big question was: "Hey, Pat, what's the 'Hey Hey' made out of?"

As if he'd been cued, McDonough walked into the room, and Pat said, "Here's the guy who should have all the answers. John, the press is asking me, what kind of material is the 'Hey Hey' made out of."

Red-faced with embarrassment, McDonough said he didn't know. In other words, the signs were a last minute effort to honor Jack in an attempt by the Cubs to save face.

* * *

Harry Caray came to Chicago because of Jack Brickhouse. After he was fired for having an affair with a daughter-in-law of the owner of the St. Louis Cardinals and almost being run down in a planned auto accident, Harry decided it was time to move on. That was when Jack helped him land the broadcasting job with the White Sox. Jack and Harry had known each other for decades and had tipped a glass or two together over the years. Having one of them on the North Side and one on the South Side was a natural. Harry took the job with the Sox and settled into the booth at Comiskey Park.

When Jack decided it was time for him to retire from doing the television play-by-play of Cubs games, it was assumed by just about everybody that Milo Hamilton would succeed him at the microphone. In fact, it was all set to happen. Jack would make the announcement on Monday that Milo would be the new play-by-play for WGN-TV.

But before this could come to pass, Jim Dowdle, who was the head of the Tribune Company's broadcasting unit, received a call from Harry who said he wanted to work for the Cubs. "Hey, Jim!" he said, "I'm box office."

Dowdle listened to him, and the day before Jack was supposed to make his announcement, he called Jack and asked him to come to the Tribune Tower that day for a little talk. After meeting with Dowdle, Jack called home and said, "Sweetheart, don't fix me a double when I get home. Fix me a triple."

On Monday, Jack dropped the bombshell that Harry would be his replacement in the booth and not Milo. Poor Milo moved on to the Astros, and Harry stayed with the Cubs until he died.

Harry Caray had no other interests once he came to the Cubs. I thought he was afraid to leave the booth. His cruddy and crude style made him popular with the fans, and the rest is history.

People now ask if Jack got a statue just because Harry got one. Pat says it's a non-issue. Everybody who knew Jack knew he was a great broadcaster and a totally committed Chicagoan. He did Cubs games on TV for more than three decades. His statue will personify that. It's only fitting that they put it on Jack Brickhouse Way adjunct to the Tribune Building on Michigan Avenue where Jack began his broadcasting career. I was there for the unveiling of the statue, and poor Pat was obviously upset. The city planners say the statue must be moved off the walkway. They already say it's an obstruction for pedestrians.

Recently, Pat had hip surgery, so perhaps she'll have the time once and for all to stop the controversy over the statue.

* * *

The good times with the White Sox were plentiful, and it was because we had quite a cast of characters on those teams in the late '70s and early '80s.

Eric Soderholm, a decent guy who could hit a little bit, was our third baseman,1977-79. He was also known for his poetry, which was read on the air during "Monday Night Baseball." Eric is now living in the suburbs of Chicago and runs a ticket agency called "The Front Row." He's raking in enough money to write poetry whenever the mood strikes.

Greg "Bull" Luzinski was our DH in 1981. Bull was always a solid hitter and a good guy who could definitely put some food away. I've never seen a guy who could devour two or three dinners and think nothing of it. One night in "The French Room" in Cleveland, Bull, Ron LeFlore, and I went through 10 bottles of wine. We drank so much that even the sommelier was getting intoxicated. We then ordered steak tartar and finished dinner. Ron and the Bull went out to party some more, and I went to my room because everything was spinning. All that food started to catch up with Bull toward the end of his career. A few years down the road, he started freezing up, and he took a couple of called third strikes, which made some people think something was wrong. Everybody thought it was his eyesight, but later everybody knew it was his chest. The team would bring a doctor into the clubhouse just in case he'd take one of those mighty swings and keel over.

Bull also had bum knees and could barely run — something that Piersall pointed out with regularity. During one particular broadcast Piersall ripped the Bull for his "cement-footedness," and said, "He's too slow. I bet I could beat him in a sprint." Soon this echoed back to the team, and Bull itched for a shot at Piersall. If he couldn't punch him out, the least he could do would be to blow him away in a sprint. Piersall was around 52 years old at the time. When Piersall caught wind of this, he made sure he was down on the field during batting practice. They were ready to race — until Veeck put a stop to it. Either way, Veeck figured, the sprint was a bad idea. He didn't want Piersall to have a heart attack, and if Piersall won, Veeck didn't want word out that Luzinski was slower than a 52-year-old broadcaster with insanity papers. After all the hoopla, Jimmy came in as usual to his locker to prepare for a fly-ball session with the outfielders. But that time,

guys had strung tape all across the face of his locker so he couldn't get in, and a doll hung down from the top with a noose around its neck. Jimmy went ballistic. Everyone knew who had done it, so we just laughed.

Don Kessinger was the player-manager this year. He told me it was going to be a long year because all he had to work with was eight DH's. We struggled defensively for sure. Don would yell things out to the pitcher from his shortstop position because every time he came to the mound it was considered by the umpire as a visit to the mound by the manager. He made the mistake a few times. He would then plead with chief umpire to give him a break. Sometimes as a base runner he would have to wave his arm to let the bullpen know who needed to start warming up. He said it was very difficult to communicate with everyone when he was on the field. He also acknowledged my dilemma with Ron Schueler as my pitching coach. He said he had to do it or the pressure was on to hire somebody after the death of the former pitching coach. Don was so capable as a manager that I'm still surprised he's not managing a big league team somewhere — like on the north side of Chicago.

It was some crew. Ralph Garr played right field in '78 and '79, and he was one of the fastest guys in baseball. Known as the "Roadrunner," he could kill you with his speed. In the outfield, though, he made easy plays look hard. He could produce a run or two for you at the plate, and cost you a run or two in the field.

Ron LeFlore was an ex-con who played center field. The Bad Boy of the White Sox could take advantage of the rules because he could hit a little bit and he sure could run. He had led the AL with 68 steals back in 1978 when he was with Detroit and the NL with 97 in 1980 when he was with Montreal. He was a pivotal character in my eventual downfall with the Sox.

Claudell Washington was another outfielder. He would just come out swinging from the heels and spray the ball to all fields. I saw him hit three homers in a game, one to left center, one to right center, and one down the line. Claudell really loved cars, especially BMWs. He'd always be good for two or three new ones during the course of a year.

Francisco Barrios was one of my closer friends on the team. I used to call him my *caballo*, which is Spanish for horse, because when we'd be in the outfield running before games, he'd prance like a horse and make a neighing sound, his long, thin black hair flowing behind him. Francisco was gone after 1981.

In 1980 we had four lefties: Tex Wortham, Ross Baumgarten, Britt Burns, and me. *Baseball Digest* did a cover story on us with the heading, "No Right-Hand Turns." As a matter of fact, our picture can be seen on the wall of Dustin Hoffman's room in the movie "Rainman." Tex took a line drive off the head in Oakland, and he was never the same after that. Baumgarten was a finesse pitcher, a guy who had good stuff but nothing overpowering. He would sit by the pool in the hotel and read The *Wall Street Journal*.

Two other pitchers, one good — Richard Dotson — and one very good — LaMarr Hoyt — would flourish and join Burns as the meat of the staff. Burns would gulp down a gallon of milk when he pitched. He was a good guy who had a big heart and the guts to match. His father was hit by a car as he was getting mail from his rural roadside mailbox and suffered severe injuries, Britt flew back to see him, then returned to the team in time to gut out his scheduled start. He threw every pitch was for his dad who lay in a coma in the hospital. It was one of the most powerful displays of strength of heart I've ever seen. Burns would have been a good one, but a hip problem cut his career short.

Hoyt was another story. He was the second coming of Catfish Hunter. Hoyt had pinpoint control and could dominate a game. He never hesitated to hold the ball a different way, just so he could throw it and see what new and exciting tricks he could make it do. Even though we were on the same team, it wasn't until 1983 when I was traded to the Cubs that I really appreciated how good he had become. As a person, he had an edge about him; he was spirited and defiant. He was easy to get along with, and his teammates liked him. He had lots of friends, and when we were playing the Orioles, they would come to visit and the party would last for days.

During spring training 1982, Jerry Koosman was scheduled to pitch three innings in an intrasquad game, Burns three, and me the last three. We had a young slugger named Ron Kittle, who went on to be a Rookie of the Year in 1983. Kittle came up against Koosman and hit a ball about 375 feet for a home run. He came up against Burns and hit one about 390 for a homer. Then against me, he hit one so far, the umpire lost sight of it as it sailed out of the park. Kittle stood there and looked at it, and the ump said, "I don't know if it was fair or foul."

I yelled back, "Hell, if a guy hits a ball that far, you should just call it a home run."

Everybody started laughing in both dugouts.

We were a staff of colts learning to become Thoroughbreds, but that was one of Mr. Veeck's great promotion jobs — convincing the fans that, even if you lose, the team can still be entertaining. Looking back, we had some very gifted ballplayers, yet so different from each other in every way that you wonder how Bill Veeck managed to put so many of them together in the same place.

The manager of this motley crew was my manager in Knoxville, a young up-and-comer named Tony LaRussa. Three weeks after Disco Demolition, he became manager on August 2, 1979.

At first, when we worked together in the minors, I liked him. His hair was kind of long, which is how you could tell if a guy was cool. He was studying to be a lawyer while he was managing Knoxville, which added a kind of academic aura to the way he ran the team. One time when we were in Montgomery, I walked by his room and his drapes were open. On one of the double beds was paper everywhere, school papers for his law studies. He impressed me then. He was someone driven enough to pursue a law degree while managing his way through the minors.

But LaRussa was young, only in his mid-30s when he was managing the Sox, and maybe partly because of that, he and LeFlore were at each other's throats. Ron and Tony were close in age, but Ron had more Major League experience. Tony was afraid of confronting LeFlore face-to-face, so he would say things about LeFlore to guys on the team and not back it up. LeFlore was always at the front of the effort to discredit Tony and cause him as much grief as possible. He would quiz Tony after the games, which I think made him a better manager; but it was humiliating in front of the other players.

On one trip, LeFlore brought a marijuana cake onto a team flight. His girlfriend from California had made the cake for him. She even served it to coaching staff. Her name was Candy, and she was right out of a cabaret nightclub. She actually took some flights on the team plane with us on a few road trips — another thing the players didn't like that LaRussa let happen. On other occasions before games, LeFlore would come in late to batting practice and everybody would say, "Oh, Ron's late again." He would be in the clubhouse, sleeping. He used to take one of the trainer's tables from the training room out into the clubhouse, and he would catch a quick pre-game nap, complete with blankets and pillows. Once in Detroit we even set up a phone and put ashtrays and old Kentucky Fried Chicken boxes next to him and took a picture, symbolizing his comfy clubhouse setup. LeFlore was lying there, snoozing, and Tony didn't say a word to him. Everybody was expecting him to shake him up and say, "Hey, get your ass up!" But he never did. Many players lost respect for him because of that.

You never knew what LaRussa was going to do. He treated players differently, which was my gripe with him. With a manager like Billy Martin, you knew what to expect. With LaRussa, you didn't.

When you have a bad apple like LeFlore, it drags everyone else down. I didn't realize it then, but the lifestyle, the drugs, and all the other things that I'd fallen into tainted my relationship with baseball. My life off the field prevented me from treating the game with the respect it deserved. Ron made things go on that weren't always good. He was a veteran, a guy who'd been around, and younger guys were fascinated by this seedy, street-smart attitude, the great athlete who can tell everyone to get screwed. You're very impressed by that when you're 23 years old and a guy tells the manager to shove it. I remember him telling LaRussa that all the time.

Because I had lost respect for LaRussa, I fell in with the person who was most against him, and that was LeFlore. The Sox knew what kind of guy Ron was, and so in 1982 they specifically instructed Dotson, Hoyt, and me not to hang around with him. I remember saying to Hoyt and Dotson once, "Hey, Ronnie and I are heading out after the game. You guys want to come?" And Dotson said, "Nah, Hoyt and I are staying away from Ronnie."

But for me, being young and rebellious, it made sense to hang out with LeFlore. When the establishment tells you not to do something, it makes you want to do it even more. Dotson severed his relationship with LeFlore, but a few other guys and I were caught up in it. From my perspective, if he was such a bad guy, they should cut him, but he was making around $800,000; there was too much money involved.

Ron knew how to order people around. He was low-key and rebellio us in every way, and he was entertaining, too. To me, hanging with Ronnie was part of being on the road, and his room was one of the sites of one of the most famous brawls in White Sox history.

In Cleveland in 1981, a bunch of us were out drinking. The Bull, Jerry Koosman, Ron Schueler, Carlton Fisk, Eddie Farmer, Francisco Barrios, Ron, and me. Frankie was a big guy, about 6-foot-5 and 230 pounds. That night Frankie had his eye on a girl who happened to be with about six other husky guys. No matter. Frankie usually took what Frankie wanted, so he started putting the moves on this girl. Eddie Farmer — who's now the Sox's radio voice — came up to me and said, "You'd better get Frankie out of here because he's going to start a fight."

That made sense, so I went up to Frankie and told him we were going to another bar. Frankie and I started walking out of the hotel, he behind me, up this long flight of stairs. All of a sudden a sharp pain shot down my back like an explosion in my spine. Frankie had kicked me with his big old cowboy boot, right in my back. I turned around and slugged him in the jaw, and we brawled up the stairs to the front of the hotel check-in. We slugged it out. He left himself open a couple of times, and I nailed him. We went at it for what seemed like an hour but was actually only 10 or 15 minutes. The bell hadn't even rung for the end of the first round when I yelled to the guy at the front desk, "Call the police! Call the police!" I knocked Frankie down with a left, then jumped on top of him. I grabbed him by his hair, then all of a sudden, Luzinski and LeFlore and everyone came up from the basement bar. All I remember saying was, "Frankie, I told you not to mess with me! I told you not to mess with me!"

The cops came and handcuffed Frankie, then he started gnawing at the three-inch chain between his wrists. I can still see him doing anything possible to get free. I ran out of the hotel and came back about four hours later. After that, everything settled down. I called Ron's room, then went up for a beer. Ron told me Frankie was in jail. I didn't know it then, but Glen Rosenbaum, known as "Rosie," the White Sox's traveling secretary, bailed him out of jail two hours later.

At about two in the morning, the phone rang in LeFlore's room, where I was hanging out because I couldn't sleep. Ron picked up the phone and said, "Yeah, Steve's here." Click. And he hung up the phone.

"Who was that?" I said.

"It's Frankie," he said. "Frankie's coming up here."

Before you know it, Ron opened the door — it was just like him to want some more excitement — and in came Frankie with a key in his hand. The keys back then weren't the credit card types they have now; these were real keys large enough to tear a hole in your pants if you sat down wrong. Frankie took this key and went right for my face. I put my left arm up in defense, and he gashed my wrist. I still have the scar to prove it. I was bleeding all over the place. I swung at him and missed and put a hole in the hotel room wall, for which LeFlore would charge me $213 later on for repairs.

We fought in the room and spilled out into the hallway. Frankie was choking me, and I punched him in the nose and broke it. Blood was everywhere. Guys were opening their hotel room doors to watch the fight. Finally, I yelled out, "Someone's going to have to help meeeeee! Someone's got to get Frank-eeeeee!"

Everybody was watching. What a show it was! Finally, we rolled our way over to the elevator, and when the doors opened, some of the guys and I pushed Frankie in and sent him to another floor. That was the end of it. Frankie was left with two black eyes and a broken nose, and I came out of it with a hand-print crushed into my neck and the cut on my left wrist. I called LaRussa at 3:35 a.m. and told him I was going home. He talked me out of it. The next day we had a team meeting about the incident, and Frankie and I shook hands.

Two days later, the papers ran post-incident pictures of me and Frankie in the paper. I wasn't the one who looked like he'd been in a fight because the photos were only head shots and my injuries weren't visible.

As it turned out, Frankie's girlfriend apparently had a thing for me. She used to call me up late at night, and I would tell her I was married. That's what started it. Frankie couldn't handle it, and that night in Cleveland he just snapped and let it all out. He had a lot of problems, a lot of addictions; however, he couldn't handle leaving baseball after his last season in 1981. Frankie committed suicide in Hermosillo, Mexico, at age 29 on April 9, 1982, a very sad day for everyone who knew him.

* * *

All of a sudden you're in pro sports and you're making a little money and you get introduced to more drugs, and then a little more, and a little more. A guy I knew nicknamed Bugsy, who had Major League experience, was the oldest guy on the Double-A team, and he was a partier. He had a van, and he and me and a few of the guys — including Hoyt, Dotson, and Rich Barnes — used that van as a party bus. We all had our own apartments and places throughout Knoxville, and I was with Sandy at the time. I remember at a team party in 1978 I was drugged with LSD. They slipped it into my drink, and I didn't even know it. I never want to feel that way again, like my head was not attached to my body. One of the pitchers on that Knoxville team said he had tripped on over 3,000 hits of acid, so he sat with Sandy and me until the drugs wore off. One game he started against Detroit, he came over to me during the first inning and said he couldn't even feel his feet hitting the ground. He would do three black beauties — 60 milligrams of speed — before his starts. Eventually, his hair began falling out. One time, he grabbed some of his hair and pulled it out with his bare hands. Freddie eventually made the Show with one of the best sliders in baseball, but his desire for chemicals hurt him. Guys did speed because it made them feel more competitive, gave them the edge or made them more alert.

Spending the days with LeFlore eventually settled into a comfortable routine. Each game, he'd make a couple of errors, maybe a stolen base, a base hit, and he'd be walking around, sniffing. He'd look the guys up and down and say, "Hey, we're going out." We'd go to his room, and he'd break something out and guys would take the mirror off the wall and roll up a $100 bill. Then we'd go out for drinks and hang out in clubs. I had sources for drugs; other guys had their sources. But with Ron being there it wasn't as if you had to look hard to find someone to party with. Some guys had their own little stash. Nobody ever charged anyone for anything. One time you bought, the next time somebody else did. It was a team effort.

One time we made a horrible appearance at the clubhouse. We left Ron's room and walked right into the clubhouse for an afternoon game. Four of us. It was pretty suspicious-looking. You realize everybody's looking at you and knows what you've done. That was the day Ron fell asleep on the trainer's table and we took the photos of him with the KFC boxes. I remember walking into the clubhouse and realizing I hadn't slept all night, and then feeling shame.

Once I went into LeFlore's room and saw front office people there. He was doing cocaine right in front of them. I did it, too. Our conduct was a major act of defiance, like a death wish. Deep down, I was probably hoping they'd confront me with what they knew. That shows how self-destructive it was for the team to bring in a guy like LeFlore. Sooner or later, the negative lifestyle grabs hold of you. We'd get home at two or three in the morning and go to bed — if we could. We'd shut the curtains real tight, sleep in, get up at two or three in the afternoon, then grab lunch.

In the last season of Tiger Stadium in Detroit, the Tigers held a special day for their great players of the past. Among them was LeFlore. After being honored, he went up in the stands and sat with Gerry Clarke, the general manager of the Cook County Cheetahs, an independent team that LeFlore managed. Clarke went for a beer and a hot dog during the sixth inning. When he returned to his seat, LeFlore was gone. Clarke wondered where his manager had wandered off to and continued to wonder through the rest of the game. When the game ended, Clarke returned to his hotel room without LeFlore. He turned on the television to watch ESPN, and there on the screen was LeFlore being escorted out of Tiger Stadium by the police. LeFlore was arrested for back child support payments. Clarke was relieved to know where his manager was.

Six or seven guys made up our group, including Hoyt. He was a very quiet, funny guy who got a lot of women with his easygoing Southern Comfort attitude. He kept a low profile. On the mound, he was one of the greatest talents ever. He had an amazing ability to do things with the baseball and understand hitters. He put on some weight, but he never seemed to care too much. He never seemed to care much about anything, really. He was the type to live for the day. Hoyt could have been one of the all-time greats, but after he was traded to San Diego, he was caught with marijuana and Valium at the Mexican border in February of 1986. His wife Sylvia had had enough and even called the police to have him arrested. Maybe she thought it would help if he got caught and then went to counseling. She knew it was killing their marriage and his baseball career. He won a civil suit against the Padres. His attorney was very smart to use a defense of insomnia because the judge ruled in Hoyt's favor. So San Diego had to pay him the rest of a huge contract because of that ruling. Hoyt's career fizzled out because his addictions got the best of him. Baseball should have something equivalent to the Betty Ford Clinic, designed for players so they can come to grips with the personal problems that accompany the baseball lifestyle.

* * *

LaRussa and I had gotten along fine from the minors and his early days with the Sox. We had seen some crazy things together in the Dominican Republic, where we played in the winter of 1980 for San Pedro de Macoris, a place where some of the game's best shortstops have come from. One day before a game Tony's wife, Elaine, came out of their room yelling and screaming that something was wrong with their white poodle. The dog, as I looked at it, was running around wildly in circles. We tried to help, but in minutes the dog was dead. We found later that the maintenance people at our small complex had put out some rat poison out that afternoon, and the dog had eaten some.

Later that season after a game, Tony, Elaine, Sandy and I were coming home in our car, when in the middle of the dark, deserted road stood a horse. Tony stopped the car with the head-lights shining right on the horse. It wouldn't move. So Tony opened his car door, walked over, and grabbed the rope hanging from the horse's neck. He spoke Spanish well, so he and I approached the first house that we saw — it was a shack, actually. Tony knocked on the door, a man answered, and there we were, two Americans standing there in the dark with a horse. "Is this your horse?" Tony asked in Spanish. The man said no and closed the door abruptly. So we left the horse there in the yard because we didn't know what else to do with it.

Many Dominicans are superstitious, and practice voodoo as a

religion. The next morning on our small beach at Punta Garza, the horse lay on the shore, dead, its neck cut by a machete. Maybe it was voodoo, maybe not. Whatever it was, it was scary. At least I didn't wake up with the horse's head in my bed. We were scared many times while we were in the Dominican Republic. People told us that, if we were ever in trouble or held up by the police, we should say, "Rafael Antoon," the team owner, and if you knew him, you were okay. We still had to be careful. Before leaving the U.S., Tony told me to make sure not to bring any marijuana with me because they'd nail you for that. Instead, I bought a copy of *High Times* magazine, so I could point to pictures of weed to let teammates know what I was hoping for.

Times were wild in the Dominican Republic, and the games were, too. I remember the fans throwing oranges and other fruit at me because I hadn't done well the time before. I took the ball, drew back my arm, and screamed, pretending I was going to whip the ball into the stands. It's fun to see a thousand people covering up their heads at the same time. The crowds were crazy. During a game, a fan stood up and peed right where he was in the stands.

These were the good times LaRussa and I had together in the Dominican Republic, but our relationship headed downhill from there. The low point was an episode in 1982 that turned us against each other for good.

My grandmother and I were best friends. She was my mom's mom, but she was also someone I could talk to, someone who understood what was going on in my head and could relate to what I was feeling. She had lived with us all my life and along with my mom had raised me into the person I was.

On May 7, 1982, my grandmother suffered a heart attack. I called Tony and asked him if I could spend the time with her instead of going to Detroit for our weekend series. She was on the critical list, and I wanted to be there with her when she was conscious and aware of who was near her. Tony said I could miss the flight to Detroit, but he wanted to see me there on Saturday so I could throw under the watch of our pitching coach, Ron Schueler. I didn't follow instructions. I stayed in Chicago. Saturday I worked out on my own at Comiskey Park. Grandma had another heart attack and wasn't doing well, but I made the trip to our next series in Toronto. They bombed me, and in the fourth inning of what would be our only loss on the trip, Tony came out and hooked me. The second I hit the dugout, I made a beeline for the clubhouse to call the hospital to check on my grandmother, to see if she was alive. LaRussa was standing right there, watching me. As soon as I hung up the phone, he barked at me, "I hope nobody else in your family gets sick because you won't be home to be with them, after the way you pitched!" I took my shoe and threw it at him, and we charged each other. Some of the guys had to come in to break up the fight.

The following Friday, May 14, a third heart attack killed my grandma. She was 83.

Tony was angry at me for missing my workout in Detroit, blowing my start in Toronto, and generally not being all there for the team. "Family comes first," Tony told the papers. "But I have to balance the needs of family with the needs of the team." That was his philosophy. This was mine: I am a human being first and a ballplayer second. I acted accordingly, and I would do the same thing again in a minute.

I resented what LaRussa did to me from then on. All I ever wanted was an apology, and I never got it. I hated him for that and did everything in my power to rebel in the face of his authority.

One time we had a doubleheader at home and I was in the bullpen, waiting for the call to relieve. Kevin Hickey — who's a story all by himself — was out there with me because we were the two lefties LaRussa would call on for relief. Hickey was a Cinderella story, a softball pitcher who had been discovered in a tryout and made it all the way to the big leagues. He always made the most of his opportunity. He used to arrive at the park every day at 2:00 p.m., when the coaches did. He always acted like he would take every day for all he could. He loved the game.

The first game went along, and LaRussa called out to the bullpen for help. Hickey and I were both warming up, then he gave the signal for Hickey to pitch. He trotted onto the field and did the job. As I sat out there, I thought, Okay, LaRussa called him for the first game, it's only logical that I'm called for the second game.

In between games, Hickey and I walked out to the bullpen, and I said to him, "Hey, if LaRussa calls you to pitch in this second game before me, I'm going to follow you right up to the mound, and then I'm going to break off and have it out with LaRussa." Hickey smiled in anticipation.

Hickey was a hell of a pitcher at that time, but it wasn't as if he had outpitched me or anything like that, so I felt I deserved a call.

The game moved into the later innings, when all of a sudden we were in trouble. LaRussa called the pen for me to start warming up. And 30 seconds later — literally, 30 seconds — he called down again and asked if I was ready. Artie Kusnyer, who was the bullpen coach and LaRussa's right-hand man, said no. While this was going on, I yelled to Artie, "Hey, I need a few more minutes, stall for me."

LaRussa decided to show me who was boss. "Tell Hickey to warm up," he said. Next thing you know, LaRussa walked out to the mound, slow as he could, and started chatting to the catcher and pitcher, taking his own sweet time so Hickey could warm up the right way. Then he called him in.

Hickey opened the big green door of the bullpen in deep center field and started toward the mound. True to my word, I went right next to him. This confused the hell out of LaRussa, and he started gesturing wildly to the bullpen as if to say, "No, not Trout. Hickey!" The fans and umpires had no idea what was happening because we are both lefties. I kept going all the way in, and when I reached the point where the shortstop was, I didn't head to the mound, I broke off to the dugout and stood on the top steps.

LaRussa yelled, "Get back to the bullpen!"

But I stood right there. If he was going to show me up, I was going to show him up. It was the principle of the thing. LaRussa walked off the mound and stomped over to the dugout. I had my arms folded, and he came up to me and said, "Get your ass back down to the bullpen."

"No way," I said, and it was a good thing he didn't get too close or we might have gotten into it right there on the field.

Hickey did a good job, as it turned out. Chicken Willie, the best clubhouse man in the game, had some good chicken that night, so I walked in there and started having my food. LaRussa came into the clubhouse and said, "That's going to cost you a hundred bucks for showing me up."

I snapped back at him between bites of chicken, "Okay, just don't spend it all in one place."

Somewhere along the way, LaRussa earned a reputation as "the thinking man's manager." Maybe it was the whole lawyer angle or that he was one of the first to use computers that made everyone think LaRussa was so much smarter than everyone else, but I just didn't see that. I guess if someone labels you a clown, you're a clown, and if someone labels you a cerebral manager, you're a cerebral manager. Think about it. LaRussa had Mark McGwire hitting 40 homers a season, Jose Canseco hitting 40 homers and stealing 40 bases, Dave Stewart winning 20 games a season, and Dennis Eckersley saving 40 games a season. With four players like that, hell, I could manage a team to a division title. It's like the Bulls' triangle offense. With Michael Jordan and Scottie Pippen, the triangle offense looks pretty damn good. But if you give the triangle offense to the LA Clippers, you wouldn't get the same results.

LaRussa wasn't smarter than anyone else. He was just an expert at synergizing a team — making it better than the sum of its parts. He took the Sox from that awful year in 1980, when we went 70-90, to a division title in 1983. But I can tell you that when LaRussa was managing the White Sox during my time there, the players gave him little respect because there was so much hypocrisy going on.

Tony has stayed in the game for a long time, and his managing style has been successful for the most part. Tony likes to keep his staff of coaches close to him. His baseball friends are called "Tony's cronies."

* * *

To me, the worst part of playing for the Sox, though, was having to deal with Ron Schueler. Now, I'll be the first to admit that he has been a decent general manager for the Sox, but some of the things that he did to me back then were uncalled for.

In 1979, my first year in the bigs, Schueler was 31. He had been a below-.500 pitcher for most of his career. In eight games that season, he had a 7.32 ERA and an 0-1 record. With so many young arms on the staff, he could see the end was near for him. Not surprisingly, we had our share of run-ins. He was a guy trying to hang on, and I was barely old enough to drink. Maybe I had the talent that he never had, I don't know. Whatever the case, in 1980, all of a sudden he was the pitching coach. What I heard was that it was a cost-cutting move by Veeck. Schueler was under contract, and they knew he couldn't make the staff. So instead of eating his salary, they made him the pitching coach and paid him for that. For the rest of my time with the White Sox, Schueler didn't teach me one thing about pitching, and I doubt if anybody else picked up much of anything from him either.

From Day One, Schueler didn't like me. One spring training, we were all done with practice and ready to do our running, and Schueler pulled everyone together at the Sox training complex. He said, "Okay, Steve, you're going to get a 100-yard start, and you've got to run around the whole complex. If anyone catches you, you have to run four extra laps." Stupid as I was, I started running, and after about 200 yards I looked back and nobody was behind me. They were laughing all the way to the showers. A practical joke can be fun, but I wasn't laughing.

Another time, we were playing at Comiskey, where the bull-pens run along the baselines. The phone rang, and Schueler answered it. After he hung up, he said, "Get up, kid! You're in next inning." I ran to the mound to start throwing, and I looked in the stands to find my friends, then pointed to myself as if to say to them, "Yes, I'm going to pitch." I turned around to see where the catcher was, and all I could see was about seven guys laughing their tobacco-stained faces off. That time I thought the practical joke had gone a little too far because he embarrassed me in front of my friends.

Schueler did a lot of small things to me, and I was concerned that we might get into a fight. So I talked to Jim Willoughby, a relief pitcher we had acquired from Boston. I asked him to talk to Schueler on my behalf. Willoughby was a veteran, and I thought it would help, but it really didn't. No matter what, Ron saw me as a hippy-type, and I saw him as a redneck.

When practical jokes go too far, you want revenge, and the way I earned revenge was by acting out. I was only 22, so I decided if the coaches weren't going to respect me, I wasn't going to respect them.

Schueler and I never talked about the philosophy of pitching. He tried to teach me a spitball. I remember one day at Comiskey Park, I was pitching against George Brett, and I looked around at all the people, took my hat off and wiped my two fingers over my sweaty forehead to make the ball wet. I threw it to the plate to see if it would sink. Schueler wanted the spitter to be my "out" pitch — the one you use to make hitters get themselves out — and as I started relying on it, it shattered my confidence in my other pitches. With this new pitch in my repertoire, I started throwing differently, but my shoulder began to hurt.

Early on I could tell I wasn't going to work out with the White Sox. After '81, a strike year, I had my first arbitration case; I was represented by my agents, the Hendricks brothers. We were making our case against the new ownership group of Eddie Einhorn and Jerry Reinsdorf, which had bought the team in January of '81.

When a case comes before an arbitrator, the team arms itself with all the stats and rhetoric it can muster so it comes out on top; your agent loads up with all the stats and impassioned pleas he can scrounge up so that you come out on top. That year I had gone

8-7 with a 3.46 ERA. I had started 18 games and finished three of them, and I had walked just 38 while striking out 54. Not great, but okay. The White Sox finished 54-52 and in the middle of the pack in the AL West. As the season had wound down, my arm started hurting, and with nothing to gain, I bowed out of a couple of starts down the homestretch. I thought that was smart, so I wouldn't risk permanent damage.

According to the White Sox, that didn't make sense. The team claimed that by bailing out the last two starts I proved I was not a "go-to" pitcher, and that I didn't take my last starts because I wanted to have a winning season. As the tide shifted back and forth during the hearing, some of the Sox representatives were really starting to score some digs at me. I asked the arbitrator if I could say a few words, and he granted permission.

I said, "I don't think anybody can challenge my integrity and my love for the game of baseball. I care about the game, and I always will. Let me just say that after one game against the Yankees this year, Reggie Jackson called up the owner of our team, Bill Veeck, and said, 'Mr. Veeck, Trout is the toughest left-hander I have ever faced.' Mr. Arbitrator, that came from a great hitter who will be in the Hall of Fame someday."

On the way out of the arbitration, Randy Hendricks looked at me and said, "You just won the case for us." He was right.

My new contract was for $250,000.

Before that game on a sunny Sunday afternoon, I was allowed to leave the Saturday night game in the third inning. On the way home, I stopped at DiCola's on Western Avenue for seafood. I spoke with the owner, a short man in a white apron. I told him I wanted a fish that would make me strong for my game against the Yankees the next day. He laughed as if to say, "Yeah, right. You're pitching against the Yankees, and I'm the Pope." He said, "Try the salmon, and I'll turn the game on tomorrow and see if you're there." He added, "If you get a chance, strike out that Reggie Jackson for me. I really hate him." I said I'd do my best against Jackson. Well, lo and behold, I struck out Reggie four times that game. Maybe that's why he called Mr. Veeck and said I was the toughest left-handed pitcher he ever faced. I went into DiCola's a week later, and Mr. DiCola gave me a box of lobster tails. He treated me like a king. He said striking out Reggie four times made him feel great.

I did do well against Reggie. One time — actually, the next time — I pitched against him in New York he met me outside the stadium by the parking lot and offered to give me a ride back to the hotel in his Rolls-Royce. I still declined the offer, but when he went into his shirt pocket and pulled out a joint, I didn't decline that offer. He handed it to me in a hand gesture like giving me five. We made the switch, and I took it back to the hotel and unrolled it. I thought since Reggie is such a winner that he might have laced it with something that would kill me. All I know is he couldn't hit me, so maybe this is it. I inspected it, and the pot inside looked like pure Hawaiian. I re-rolled it and headed out on the town.

The 1982 season started bad and got worse. Snow was flying in April in Chicago, so our home-opening series was canceled. We started our season with three days of practice at the Metrodome in Minnesota to prepare for a four-game series in New York. I wasn't in the rotation that series, so one night I went to Rusty Staub's restaurant with LeFlore, Koosman, and Jerry's friend from the Italian section of New York, a guy who had big shoulders and no neck. We left Rusty's and went to a nightclub, where we found Schueler and Art Kusnyer, the bullpen coach and a very muscular guy. Kusnyer came up to me and grabbed my arm tightly, and I broke away from him. "Head to the hotel, Trout," he said. I really didn't want a confrontation, especially on the opening series of the year. So I told Koosman's friend that I had to leave and it was nice to have met him. He wanted to know why I was leaving. I told him exactly what happened. He went up to Kusnyer and said, "If you touch Trout again, I'll break your arms." Artie left me alone the rest of the night.

This was not the way to start the season.

As if having the manager and the pitching coach against me wasn't enough, I compounded the problems when I went to the coaches and told them I didn't want to throw to Carlton Fisk. If you know anything about Fisk, you know that he's the slowest son of a gun to ever strap on a mask and shin protectors. He would stand up, adjust his jock, fix his mask, and pound his mitt, then drop into his crouch and give the signs; and if there were problems anywhere along the way, he'd walk ever-so-slowly out to the mound and the routine would start all over again.

In 1981, the year Fisk came to Chicago from Boston, the Red Sox saw their concession revenue decline because he wasn't there to create hot-dog breaks and stretch the game out. That's a fact. No, Fisk wasn't a ham — not like Tom Paciorek, a Mr. Pretty Boy who would take his helmet off and run his hands through his hair when he reached second or third base. I just didn't like Fisk, and I especially didn't like pitching to him. I see him running for public office in the near future. He does seem to stay away from the game now that he's retired.

He's a Hall of Famer, and he should be. But in my opinion — and you can find others who will agree with me — the man was brutal as a handler of pitchers. The first game I ever threw to Fisk, the first batter came up to the plate, and I knew what I would throw. A fastball. Standard operating procedure. That's what I always threw, and that's what any other catcher would signal to throw. Fisk gave me the signs. One and then a wiggle, and I'm in my windup. As I was making the pitch, I saw his fingers still moving. It threw me off. He did this the whole game. As a pitcher, you have no flow, no tempo going. I couldn't believe it. I was then trying to let him know the signs for what I wanted to throw, and things got screwy. But he wasn't about to change for me. It was his way of calling a game. He was going to do it his way, no matter who was pitching. Maybe that's what he feels made him so great. I don't know.

But about three starts into the 1982 season, I decided that was it. I was the first guy who asked to have Marc Hill, our backup, catch me. When I made that request, it was like I had insulted the Lord himself. Everyone said, "He's going to be a Hall of Fame catcher! Why wouldn't you want to pitch to him?" And I said, "He's too slow, he's throwing off my rhythm."

On team flights, Fisk always wore Nike apparel. I once told him that he should break down and spend some money on real clothes. For his Hall of Fame induction, I was surprised to see him giving his acceptance speech in regular clothes instead of Nike outfit.

They actually gave me Marc Hill for a while, but then they put me in the bullpen and pretty much wrote me off after that.

Oddly enough, at one point the following season, in 1983, LaMarr Hoyt complained about pitching to Fisk, and after that, Fisk didn't catch him as much. In 1983, Floyd Bannister also started requesting Marc Hill. But because I was the first and because Fisk was the gate attraction at the time, the hammer came down on me. I was soon on my way from the South Side to the North Side.

	1	2	3	4	5	6	7	8	9	R	H	E
Visitor	0	0	0	1	0							
Home	1	0	2	1	0							

The Friendly Confines

I loved playing for the Cubs.

It all started with a phone call from Wally Phillips, a radio personality at WGN, who called me at 8:15 in the morning the day I was traded and asked me how it felt to be traded to the Cubs. I told him I wasn't sure yet, since he was the first one to inform me of the trade. I put on some cross-country skis and went out for a two-hour trek through the woods that morning.

I'd become sure that nothing equals pitching at Wrigley Field. The ivy and the old brick wall and the intimacy — it is the essence of baseball, what the game can be at its finest. The wonderful old park is partly what makes the Cubs such a special team.

Playing for the Cubs has its perks. When I was playing, I often had to race to the park because I lived 60 miles from Wrigley Field, and at that time I didn't leave myself enough travel time. I'd stock my trunk with autographed items — balls, bats, caps — signed by Billy Williams, Ryne Sandberg, other guys on the team. When a cop would pull me over, I'd tell them I was a pitcher for the Cubs, throw in "the Gift of the Day," and be on my way. If my auto-graph didn't do, then a Sandberg or a Williams did.

This mobile Cubs Specialty Store came in handy more than a couple of times. One night I was leaving my sister's house in the south suburbs of Chicago around three in the morning. As I drove home, I decided I wanted to smell good for Sandy, so I put some cologne on my neck. The bottle spilled all over my lap and started to burn, seeping through my pants, so I took them off. Then — remember, it was 3:00 a.m. — I got this crazy idea to drive home naked. I slowed down to make a right turn but rolled through the stop. Before I knew it, a cop was after me. He put his lights on and pulled me over. I hurried to put my pants on, but he was concerned that I was going for a gun or something. So he approached my car very cautiously. He took my license, and after a long delay, he came back to the car and said, "We'll have to wait here. I called up the sergeant and told him I'd pulled over Steve Trout. He's on his way over to get a ball signed by you. He's one of your biggest fans." So there I was, half-naked and a little tipsy, waiting for the sergeant. By the time he arrived about an hour later, I was ready to sign anything he had. We discussed the pitching staff, the team, and the management. About a half hour later, I was free to go, laughing all the way home.

So what if the Cubs haven't won a World Series since 1908? People love them, in part because of two identities they cultivate. One is day baseball. No big deal? Well, think about it. In April, May, and September, kids are in school. They come home, the parents are at work, so they have the house to themselves — or Mom lets them turn on the TV. What's on in the afternoon? Cartoons, soaps, and the Cubs. They can also watch the games in the summer without missing their bedtime. Today, it's become a cable package. Almost half the games are on a Chicago cable channel, the rest on WGN. Let's face it; it's all about money. As the great Willie Stargell of the Pirates said to me one night, "Steve, when I go fishing, I use the best bait there is, the green lure. It catches anything you want." He was rubbing his fingers together, the international symbol for money.

Debate advertising strategies and market share all you want, you can't deny that kids are where it's at. Kids watch the Cubs on TV nationwide, and 10 years later, they're fighting for bleacher tickets or moving into the box seats. When the Cubs are on a West Coast swing, a rousing ovation greets them every time they score. Transplanted Cubs fans and kids who grew up watching the team are making all the racket, and they're everywhere. Day baseball in the heat of summer may have cost the Cubs a few pennants through the years, but it sure has helped at the box office. Now, the team has it both ways, with mostly day games and the addition of night baseball in the late 1980s.

The other Cub identity? The lovable losers. The players, coaches, and management have wanted to win through the years; but for one reason or another, they haven't. You'd think after not having won a World Series in 90 years that the fans would grow sick of it all and give up. But that hasn't happened. People wear the team's failure proudly, like a favorite tattoo.

If the Cubs win a World Series one of these years, it would be a curse for the franchise from the Tribune Company's point of view. Success will create the expectation of more success, and in modern era baseball, success costs money. Keeping the team a contender or a loser is fine with the owners because of the love affair among the fans for the ballpark and the surrounding neighborhood. Winning a World Series would only raise the bar — and the payroll.

The Cubs serve as an uplifting force for the nation, a pacifier for the masses. When life is bad in the dumps, they can all take solace in the fact that no matter how bad your life is, the Cubs are out there, failing more miserably and drawing more attention than you ever will. That's why all the Cub fans sang with Harry Caray during the seventh-inning stretch. No matter how bad your voice is, it's still better than Harry's.

Harry singing "Take Me Out to the Ball Game" started in 1975 when he was doing the White Sox games for Bill Veeck. Harry sang the song because he said it was the only song he knew all the words to. One day Veeck heard Harry singing as the organist, Nancy Faust, was playing the song. Harry was singing the words off the air, and only Veeck and the producer could hear him. The next night, without Harry knowing it, Veeck hid a public address mike in the booth, and when Harry sang the song, his voice began to be heard by all the fans in the park. That's when singing along with Harry started. Veeck said that he knew that everybody would join in singing with Harry because their voices were probably as good, if not better, than Harry's.

The tradition continues with selected celebrities singing "Take Me Out to the Ball Game" during the seventh inning stretch. This is a great marketing ploy. The Cubs have brought in personalities such as David Copperfield, Mike Ditka, and others. They just add to the charm of Wrigley Field, a place many people call "the biggest singles bar in the country."

This mentality on the North Side was where I landed after the White Sox had grown tired of my act. My "relationship" had worn thin with LaRussa and the management, so they traded me. In 1983, I was pitching in Wrigley, while the Sox were on their way to winning the American League West. Some people say the Sox won it because they got rid of a couple of bad apples, including me and LeFlore. But that didn't bother me. The Cubs also had the makings of a good team, and we had an on-the-ball general manager running the show in Dallas Green.

I needed some stabilization because my first year with the Cubs was all about transition. Dallas Green and Billy Connors gave me that and contributed to a peace of mind I'd never felt with the White Sox. They seemed genuine about wanting me to tap into my talent and strive to be a better pitcher.

They saw what I needed, and it helped me to see what I needed. All through my career, the word "potential" was strapped to my back like a grand piano, and every time I had pitched for the White Sox or the Cubs, Harry Caray made sure to mention it on the air. "He's got *so much* potential," Harry used to say in one breath, and then in the next breath, he'd wonder why I wasn't fulfilling it. Dallas didn't hold that against me. He was concerned more about who I was as a person, how I was doing and what I could contribute to the team, and less about what everybody else was saying and feeling about me.

For those who don't know him, Dallas Green could best be described as a "baseball guy." He broke into the Majors as a right-hander with the Phillies in 1960, then ended up bouncing around from the Washington Senators to the Mets and back to the Phillies before wrapping up his career in 1967.

I don't know if it was because Dallas had been a pitcher, but for some reason, he decided he was going to take me under his wing. He was, and is, the consummate baseball professional. He knew talent, the game, and how to handle people. He was a player's man and someone I always liked to talk to — and still do. I liked Dallas a lot.

If Dallas had one shortcoming, it was that he surrounded himself with his friends. Scouts, front-office people — anybody who was Dallas's friend could be found working for the Cubs, which was fine because baseball works that way. Generally, many teams in sports operate this way. But some of Dallas's friends were a little off-center or just plain couldn't do their jobs the right way. I don't believe Dallas wanted a bunch of yes-men around him, but he realized how difficult it is to find good, trustworthy people to work with.

One guy we had, Charlie Fox, was Dallas' right-hand scout. He used to stay up late when we were on road trips, thinking about the game. On one trip to Montreal, we bumped into each other as I was out having a croissant. "Kid, " he said, "I couldn't sleep. I was up all night thinking about what to do with you."

I told him, "You're sure not going to get a lot of sleep thinking about me, Charlie. You'd better get that out of your head right away."

Charlie was also into the psychic kind of stuff, biorhythms, astrology, and martial arts, and he took it all seriously. After Lee

Elia was fired in the middle of the 1983 season, Charlie was named manager for the last 39 games. We were sitting around the clubhouse before one game in Charlie's reign, and we asked why Warren Brusstar wasn't getting his innings in. Charlie said, "It's because Warren's biorhythms are down." During one of my starts in Philadelphia, Charlie looked up at Billy Connors and said, "I've seen enough of Trout. Get a reliever up." It was the first inning, and I was doing fine. He pulled me after that inning. I was furious, and so was Billy. I ran into his office, kicked over his chair, and used his phone to book a flight out of Philly. But with the whole game to calm down, I thought better of it and decided to stay. Charlie wasn't one of my favorite managers; well, it's hard for me to even call him a manager.

With all that going for us, it's easy to see why nobody thought that storied 1984 season could happen. After '83, I highly doubt that anyone could have predicted the Cubs to win the National League East in '84. But this is where you have to give a lot of credit to Dallas.

When Gary "Sarge" Matthews and Bobby Dernier came from Philadelphia in the spring of 1984, they had an immediate positive effect on the team. They walked in, and the feeling of winning started. I know I felt it. The Sarge had a presence that meant business, and Dernier had the same.

This was when I started to understand what a winning attitude was all about. With Sarge and Bobby on board, we were ready to change the things we needed to in order to win. Later, Dallas brought in Dennis Eckersley and Rick Sutcliffe. Strong personalities pervaded the clubhouse, and that wasn't entirely a bad thing. One time Sutcliffe and I squared off in the locker room because he was trying to run the team. "Come to the park and be ready to work out when Billy's ready," he told me.

"When I come to the park is none of your business," I said. We got up out of our chairs and squared off. We were going to go to blows, but Gary Matthews intervened.

Before too long, we started piling up wins. We were having fun, too, and along the way we nurtured a wonderful romance with the Chicago fans. You'd expect no less with the personalities and characters on that team.

Sarge was the left fielder and a fan favorite. He used to salute the fans in the left field bleachers as he trotted out at the start of each inning. He'd become my closest friend on the team. Ron Cey, the third baseman, was "The Penguin." Everybody had a nickname. Keith Moreland, the right fielder, was "Zonk." He had a nice bat, and while he wasn't a great outfielder, you knew he wouldn't let you down either. Right field in Wrigley is the toughest position, and Moreland was one of the better ones out there, always giving all he had. Keith and Jody Davis were inseparable. They memorized the Budweiser code of excellence printed on the bottle labels. They'd recite it word for word *a cappella*. It was as if they were getting ready for a Budweiser commercial.

There was a lot of partying on the road trips, and often the booze was flowing. We'd pass around a bottle of wine on the bus for anyone who wanted a slug, like winos do. The guys would get a little liquored up and start yelling out negative things about "The Preacher Man" or Harry Caray. (We called Jim Frey "The Preacher Man" because his size and his sermons were preacher-like.) Guys would never say anything to Harry to his face when they were sober, but when we were together on the team bus, they felt no fear to yell out unflattering remarks since they were in a group. Most players had a certain amount of animosity toward him because of his judgmental style of broadcasting. He had his favorites and always said good things about them on the air. Sandberg and Jody Davis, for example. The other guys were often the objects to his vitriolic sarcasm.

Leon Durham was "The Bull" at first base. Sutcliffe was "The Red Baron." My nickname was "Rainbow" for obvious reasons. Dernier was "Deer," the speedy center fielder and a pitcher's best friend who could catch everything from a blooper behind second base to a shot hit up against the ivy. Our catcher was Jody Davis, who back then was hitting the tar out of the ball. Sut, Davis, and Moreland liked to hang out together; Eckersley, Scott Sanderson, Ed Lynch — who was the Cubs GM in the late '90s— and Brian Dayett were pals. Leon Durham and Lee Smith were inseparable. Bobby Dernier and I were close. Chris Speier and Ryne Sandberg and some of the younger guys hung together.

Ryno, in my mind, was the best second baseman of all time. His success was a direct result of the way he approached the game. The media and the fans complained that Ryno was withdrawn, that he was hard to pin down as a person. He never wore his emotions on his uniform sleeve. Sure, he was a practical joker. He liked to put bubble bath in the whirlpool or light guys' shoe-strings on fire with rubbing alcohol; stuff like that. He played cards, and he fit in with the guys. Sandberg had a sense of humor, but it was his own for sure. He had a distinguished sort of laugh, and he laughed a lot, but never before a game.

On the field, he was all business, a baseball-playing machine. The players and coaches knew exactly what Ryno was about because he was consistent, every single day. The players all respected him because he played hard, and he played hurt. When he did visit the training room, it wasn't for long. His pain tolerance level was very high. I saw Ryno put his feet in a bucket of ice water after a game and just leave them there. Most players wouldn't be able to stand the sharp cold pain after a while, but he could just sit there and take it, putting his mind somewhere else while his feet were turning blue.

As a pitcher, you loved to have Ryno behind you. His range was great, although I didn't see him hit the ground too many times, either. Maybe it's because he made the tough plays look easy. He really did. If he got close to a ball, he'd get it. Once in Atlanta I had a no-hitter going when the ball was hit to Sandberg. He shuffled over to his right, knocked the ball down, picked it up, and threw to first, but the guy beat it out. I looked up to the scorer, who ruled it a base hit, and I started yelling, "F--- you! F---you!" A while later the commissioner sent me a nice letter stating that people can read lips, that my outburst to the official scorer was a very unpleasant exhibition, and if it ever happened again, I'd be fined.

A lot of people thought the play was an error. But Ryno had the luxury of being the consummate professional. Most of the time, the home player will get the hit call. It has to be a real blunder to be called an error at home.

Make no mistake, though. Ryno saved a pitcher's hide count-less more times than he lost it. I asked him one time what he'd tell a young kid about how to get better?" He said, "Each and every day, with each practice, try to get a little better."

That advice reminds me of my grandfather telling the story about a young boy on a farm. A cow gave birth to a calf, and the father told the boy to go out and pick up that calf every day. So he did. After a number of months, the boy realized that he was no longer picking up a baby calf but he was lifting a cow. Life's strengths are in the habits we discipline ourselves to do.

That was Sandberg's approach to the game. Also, it's an un-ending quality he has. He *did* gct better every day, and each and every year as well, unlike some people who try to do it all in one day. His numbers speak for themselves. On top of it all, he didn't really even try to hit home runs until Jim Frey said, "Hey, you know you can hit more home runs. In certain situations, when the count is 2-and-1 or 3-and-1, why don't you try to jack the ball out?" He tried it, and he hit more home runs. He didn't even try to hit homers until they opened his eyes up in 1985.

Yet as different as Ryno was to me, we had something in common. We found it difficult to perform when we had emotional troubles swirling in our heads. Ryno's emotional troubles were caused largely by his first wife, Cindy.

Guys on the team always had the suspicion that Cindy was a "friendly" girl, so to speak. She was a lively, fun-loving straw-berry blonde who always hung right on Ryno's shirt tail or his coat sleeve, making sure she was in the picture a lot. Maybe she just wanted to give the impression she was an accessible woman, but a few other guys on the team and I didn't want to end up close enough to the situation to find out. Other than some rumors and locker room gossip, a birthday party one pre-season was the only occasion that formed my opinion of the former Mrs. Sandberg.

Vicki Dernier, Bob's wife, and Cindy celebrated their birth-days at Sandberg's house, a beautiful place in the Mesa-Chandler area near Phoenix. For a present, we ordered a male stripper, and when the guy arrived, everybody moved into the living room. The stripper put the chairs side-by-side for the birthday girls, and he started doing his dance and taking his shirt off. The music was going, and everybody was smiling at them because, after all, it's a bit embarrassing to have a half-naked guy hopping around in front of you as a room full of people look on. So to fit in with the occasion, I started taking pictures, for posterity. Well, the stripper went down to his G-string, dancing in front of them, waving his hips and everything else right in front of their faces. Vicki and Cindy didn't even look embarrassed. They didn't turn their heads, but kept looking straight ahead, taking a nice long stare at their present. I was taking pictures and not noticing what was going on. Two songs later, when I took my eye out of the view-finder on the camera, the fourth song had started, and almost everybody had left the room, embarrassed. Nobody remained except me, Vicki, Cindy, and the stripper. It was a strange scene, so I turned the music off and told the guy to leave because he had overstayed his welcome. I sure would have been embarrassed if that had been my wife. You'd hope your wife would think the joke was over after a couple of dances, but these two girls didn't want to move. They were enjoying every last second of it. That was the writing on the wall to me.

Cindy was a flirtatious woman who probably wasn't the best person and definitely wasn't the best girl for Ryno, and the rumors about Cindy and the Latin players on the Cubs? I don't really know much about that stuff, although I've heard a lot of things. When Ryno was out on the road, she supposedly hit the clubs. I've been hit with so many misguided and incorrect attacks that I'm reluctant to speculate on something unless I know for sure. But after awhile, you know, if it looks like a duck, walks like a duck, and quacks like a duck, it's probably a duck.

I was sitting in box seats behind the visitors' dugout with a guy I'd met at a charity golf outing at a Sox game at Comiskey Park. Tampa Bay was in town, and when my friend saw Davey Martinez, he yelled out, "Hey, Davey, how's Cindy Sandberg doing?" I was shocked. Martinez looked up in the stands and saw me sitting with this loudmouth. I was really embarrassed because Davey and I had been teammates. I lost all respect for this guy and no longer talk to him.

The situation wore Ryno down to the nub. Even he, an emotionally impenetrable rock of a man, couldn't play through something as emotionally devastating as what was happening to him. Did his play suffer? You'd better believe it. The entire year before he retired in June of 1994 he wasn't the same player. The media and the fans might have thought he was just growing older or slowing down, but it was the mental side, not the physical, that was eating away at him. He was able to play every day, but the smile was gone.

Larry Bowa had a big influence on Sandberg. He took Ryno under his wing and helped him become not only a great player but also how to protect himself from all the jock-sniffers. Bowa helped create the Sandberg that people know as the guy who says very little and is very aloof.

So rather than be half the man and player he really is, he retired. Ryno told everyone it was because he was unhappy and feeling down, but I think it was more than that. A small part of it was he wanted to stick it to Cindy by tearing up his huge contract, breaking off their marriage, and signing a new one so she wouldn't be entitled to the money. A large part of it was so he could pull back, relax, spend some time with his children, and set his life in order.

When he came to the Cubs Convention in January of 1995, everybody was talking about how good he looked. Most of the trouble was Cindy, and that goes to show you how emotional problems can affect your life. People aren't faucets. We can't turn our lives on and off. He came back and played again because above all, Ryno's a winner. He wasn't the same player, but you can't blame him for wanting to try to return to the post-season, especially with the way 1984 and 1989 playoffs were such let-downs.

* * *

That year of 1984 all the pieces were in place, thanks mostly to Dallas, who stood by the team, and by me, through everything we went through. Thanks largely to him, this was a special time for me, because people had always thought of me as the misguided son of a guy named "Dizzy." Winning, as I found out in 1984, is the most direct route to gaining respect. As we started to move up the ladder in the NL East, people began to acknowledge that maybe this eccentric left-hander named Trout could pitch a little bit. That magic season of 1984 marked one giant leap for me as a person and a pitcher. I went 13-7 in 31 starts, and my ERA was a respectable 3.41.

More than ever I wanted to win, not just for Frey and his side-kick, third-base coach Don Zimmer, but especially for Dallas. You knew he was on your side. When there was talk some-times of Dallas maybe taking over as manager, I was one of the guys who hoped that would happen. Some times when I'd be on the mound, I'd look up into the VIP box to see if Dallas was there. I'd look back to the field and the infield grass, which was always left tall when I was pitching, and I'd say to myself that I wanted to do well for Dallas because he'd put so much trust in me. He was the first person in the Majors who truly supported me and was patient as I matured. He'd need that patience during my first season in the National League. I started off not so great, but in my third start, I beat Montreal, going eight and a third innings. After the game, the hotel we were staying at sent a special basket of fruit and wine with a letter congratulating me and offering me a free meal in the hotel restaurant. It was certainly appreciated.

Later in the season, I beat St. Louis, 10-1, throwing a four-hitter. But in the second half, I went 3-7 and only made it into the seventh inning three times in 14 starts. I ended the year in the bullpen and not talking to the media.

Thankfully, 1984 was a new start, for more than one reason. My entire perspective changed on November 15, 1983, when my daughter Taytum came into the world. Her arrival was a month early. It was the winter before the '84 season, and I was building a relationship with our new manager, Jim Frey, and his staff — something that wasn't easy after what had happened with Schueler and the Sox.

Getting over your demons isn't easy, but Billy Connors, my pitching coach, was the key. I flew down to Tampa to meet with him to get ready for the season. He picked me up at the airport and introduced me to his neighbors, Bob and Jane Tatum. They made dinner, and I mentioned that Taytum was a name we liked for a daughter, if we were going to have one. Minutes after dinner was served, the hospital called. Sandy was giving birth, eight months pregnant. I jumped on a plane right back to Chicago, and all I could think was, I'm going to be a father, I'm going to be a father.

A friend picked me up at the airport, and we ran out to a bar for a drink or two because I was so nervous, and then I said, "Let's get to the hospital."

Taytum's arrival was one of my fondest times because everything seemed to be coming into balance. I was taking yoga and had just started studying martial arts. David Katz, the martial arts teacher, became a friend of mine. I worked out a routine that was similar to pitching, using five-pound weights on my arms and legs and doing movements. I was so strong after three and a half months that my discipline, flexibility, and self-esteem were all better. I was becoming one with my family and with myself as a pitcher, and I began thinking about some important questions like, "What am I going to do to be better as a person and a pitcher?" My concentration and focus improved.

Taytum's birth was like finding a reason to live. It gave me a sense of adulthood, commitment, maturity. You have this person who's going to be seeing you and wanting to emulate what you do and who you are. Just the thought that you're a father, that makes you wake up. She was a gift. My life was to be more disciplined, my marriage stronger. No, I wasn't completely a new person. It's a long, slow process to change 10 or 15 years of your life. But it changed me. I cut out some friends who were bad influences on me. They were people on the outside of the game. I started to see and feel the change. It's like being on a health food diet. You get rid of the bad food, then you start to feel and look better. That's what happened to me. The changes I made were having a positive effect on me, and I started feeling better about myself.

I went to visit Billy Connors in Florida twice in the months leading up to the 1984 season. We went over films of 1983, and more than that, Billy worked with me on my attitude. "If you came down here to screw around, get on a plane and go home," he said. "I'm tired of your B.S. You've got a wife and baby to work for now." He was right, and I did work. Billy helped me make my mind strong, and I worked at keeping my body strong. In the months leading up to 1994, I worked on Nautilus machines to increase my flexibility and endurance. I took karate to bring the whole package together. When spring training started, I was ready.

Our new manager that season, Jim Frey, said that I had the best stuff of any pitcher — for us or against us — the entire spring.

That wasn't the only news of spring training. Before we opened camp, an astrologer was quoted in the paper as saying we'd have "fighting and turmoil in the clubhouse early in the season." Sure enough, on March 20, Dick Ruthven, one of our pitchers, and Mel Hall, one of our center fielders, slugged it out like a couple of champs. It was one of the best baseball fights I've seen.

A week later we had some more turmoil, but it was the good kind. Dallas traded Bill Campbell, one of our pitchers, and Mike Diaz, a catcher, to the Phillies for Gary Matthews, Bob Dernier, and Porfi Altamarino, a pitcher. Upon hearing about the trade, Mel Hall said, "Gentlemen, Bob Dernier does not qualify." Deer started the season in center field, and soon after, Hall was traded. Sarge was installed in left, which moved Bull Durham to first and Bill Buckner to the bench. Buckner was the most selfish player I ever played with. He was determined to be Top 10 in one statistical category, and he chose doubles. Since he was a singles hitter, he'd try to stretch as many singles into doubles as he could or he'd hold up at second instead of trying for a triple.

Before the opener, Dallas called everyone together and talked to us about what it takes to be a winner. He was furious with the way we had folded after the All-Star Break in 1983, and he said he expected more out of the veterans. This season, he said, we were going for the National League East pennant, and anyone who wasn't going to reach for the sky shouldn't bother suiting up for the Cubs that year.

I, among others, took that to heart, and step by step, we started to believe in ourselves. In our home opener on April 13, we played the Mets, who had won six straight games and had a hard-throwing rookie named Dwight Gooden. In Doc's second major league start, we hammered him for six runs. I pitched a complete game, and we won, 11-2. I even got a hit on a bunt they mis-played.

We moved into first place for the first time on April 24. Richie

Hebner hit a ninth-inning homer, and we beat St. Louis, 3-2. When the Phillies lost to the Pirates, we had a half-game lead. One month later we swept the Braves in a doubleheader, the first time the Cubs had swept a doubleheader in three years. The next day, May 25, we traded Bill Buckner to Boston for Dennis Eckersley.

Why someone didn't come up with the idea to use Eck as a reliever back then, I'll never know. But as it turned out, we kept winning anyway. Some of my best pitching came when we really needed it. On May 30, our opening day starter, Ruthven, was on the disabled list and one of our other starters, Scott Sanderson, had back spasms. So I went out and pitched seven and two-thirds innings of shutout ball, and we beat the Braves, 6-2, to stop a four-game losing streak.

After this series, we were off to New York. On getaway day, we had to rush to catch our plane, a 727 that was being held up for us. We all boarded, and I took a seat on the left side of the plane toward the rear. As the plane taxied out to the runway, I felt a lot of heat through my shoes. I called the flight attendant and asked her about it. She bent down and touched the carpet and said, "Oh, that is hot." I asked her to get the pilot, and she did. The plane stopped, and he came back to my seat. I said I thought it might be the hydraulic system causing the heat. He went back to the cockpit and called for a mechanic to come check it out. Then he announced that we'd have at least a one hour delay. There was a lot of griping about that, but it was better to be an hour late than not get there at all. As it turned out, the hydraulic system was the problem. After they fixed it, the pilot came back to my seat again and said, "Now would you like to fly the plane?" I laughed, grabbed a beer, and felt like I really did save the season.

As May rolled into June and July, we began to understand the difference between winning and being a winner. Dallas made sure we had some help along the way. On June 13, he traded away some of the team's future so we could win in the present. He shipped Mel Hall and three minor leaguers — one named Joe Carter — to Cleveland for Rick Sutcliffe, Ron Hassey, and George Frazier.

Anyone who saw Sut pitch that summer knows what it means to be a pitcher rather than a thrower. Sut worked the plate in and out, changed speeds, did whatever he could to keep hitters guessing. His motion was slow and deliberate, every time, regardless of whether he was coming with a fastball, curve or a change. I remember Frey telling Sut, "On a 3-and-2 count, why throw your fastball when you can throw a curve? Hitters are sitting on a fastball in that situation, and your curve will fool the hell out of them." Sut had a lot of success with that, and with his addition to the staff, we were as solid as any rotation in baseball that season. Eckersley told me one time that he was glad Sutcliffe was receiving all the attention, too, because it allowed us to have more of a behind-the-scenes approach to our own jobs.

Even though Sutcliffe had a pretty good career with the Cubs, I was shocked when the Cubs put him on "The Walk of Fame," considering his record in Chicago was 82-65 over eight seasons.

One game in particular defined our regular season that year. On June 23, we played the Cardinals in one of those perfect, sun-splashed summer Saturday afternoon games at Wrigley. We had 38,079 fans in the stands and a national audience on NBC. I started and lasted only three innings or so, and from then on, the game was one of those crazy back-and-forth affairs where if you missed five minutes on the radio, the lead and the flow could change three times. We fell behind, 7-1, and then, 9-3. When the ninth inning came, we were down, 9-8, and Ryno was at the plate. The Cards had sent in Bruce Sutter, a former Cub who was the most dominant reliever in the league at that time. His split-finger fastball would come at you, knee-high, and then plummet off the table about four feet from the plate. It was one of the toughest pitches in baseball at the time. Ryno stepped into the box, the game on the line, and with one mighty swing took Sutter to the bleachers and tied the game, sending it into extra innings. The fans went bonkers, jumping up and down and hugging each other. In the 10th, though, St. Louis scored two more times, and we were deflated. People were surprised if Sutter blew a save twice a month, much less twice in one day. But Ryno came up again, in the 10th, with a man on base and Sutter still on the mound. He cranked another homer to tie the game for us, 11-11. We won it in the 11th, 12-11. After the game, the Cards manager, Whitey Herzog, said, "Sandberg is the best player I have ever seen." From then on, that would become known in Cubs lore as "The Ryno Game." That game to me was the one that gave us the belief that we could win it all.

That season we just did whatever it took to win. At the All-Star break, I was 9-3 and leading the staff with 103 innings. During our West Coast swing right after the break, I had some blister problems, something that followed me throughout my career. This one was on my middle finger. I pulled the blistered skin off to expose the area underneath to the air. That sent Frey through the roof. He was furious that I had gone against conventional wisdom, which was to leave the skin on and let it heal like that. He probably figured it was just Trout, trying to find a way to throw a fly in the ointment again. But I had seen so many blisters on my hands by this point, I knew what I was doing. After pulling the skin off, I soaked the sore area in pickle juice, something Nolan Ryan had been doing for years. When we were in San Francisco, I rubbed crab shells on it. The salt in the shells helped toughen it up.

By the way, eating crabs is one of my favorite things to do in San Francisco. One day I decided to buy crabs for the guys to eat after the game. I wrapped them up in brown paper bags and put them in the bottom of the ice box in the middle of the locker room. We had a long game, and because it was getaway day, we had to hurry to catch our plane after the game was over with. I left the crabs in the icebox, and it was also getaway day for the Giants. The normal procedure is for the visiting clubhouse manager to leave the locker room unattended and turn out the lights until the home team comes back from its road trip. The clubhouse manager later told me that, when he went into the locker room after the Giants' 12-day road trip was over, the smell of the rotten crabs was so bad that Atlanta had a few members of its team get sick from the stench. I don't think the Braves won a game that series.

When we returned home to play the Dodgers the next week, July 12, the hand felt fine. I worked into the fourth inning before running into trouble. Bill Russell, their shortstop, doubled. I walked Pedro Guerrero, then got Mike Marshall to hit a line shot to Moreland in right. My mind wasn't where it should have been, and the next guy up, Candy Maldonado, singled, and the Dodgers had a run. At this point, Frey had seen enough. Usually, he'd send Billy Connors to the mound to find out what my deal was. But on this day, he was in a foul mood. He'd given up chew that day and needed somewhere to send his aggression. I was the perfect place.

Frey came out to the mound and showed me his command of the four-letter fastball. He told me to stop pitching like I was ready to go home. He said there was nobody in the bullpen waiting to come in and save me, and that he was going to leave me out there to self-destruct if I didn't get my act in gear. He said he was tired of my crap and to snap out of it. So I did. I got the next two guys out and went eight innings. I didn't get a decision, but we did go on to win, 3-2, on another game-winning homer by Ryno.

When a team gets on a roll, things just start to happen, and you get the feeling a pennant was meant to be. On July 29, I pitched a complete game against the Mets to open a doubleheader in New York. Sanderson won the nightcap. A few days later, on August 1, we moved back in front of the Mets atop the East with a 5-4, 12-inning win over the Phillies. The day after that we got some help. We led the Expos, 3-2, in the ninth, but they had runners on first and third with one out. Pete Rose slammed a line drive up the middle, but it bounced off Lee Smith's rear end. Our shortstop, Dave Owen, caught it on the fly and threw to first for a double play. On August 8, we finished a sweep of the Mets in a four-game series, and after that, it was a matter of time.

In late August, Frey gave Moreland a few days off, and he returned in a doubleheader against the Reds and hit a single, two doubles, a triple, and a homer with six RBIs, and we took the twinbill from Cincinnati.

We clinched the NL East title on September 24 in Pittsburgh, the Cubs' first title of any kind since 1945, the year my dad beat them in the World Series. Sutcliffe picked up his 16th win against one loss that night, and Chicago went crazy. People ran wild in the streets outside Wrigley Field and the party was on.

We were also running wild in the clubhouse; the party was on there, too. I never saw such a big smile on Dallas Green's face. Players were spraying as much champagne as they were drinking it. The lockers were taped up with plastic to protect them. Everybody became a target for being doused with champagne. Nobody was safe. I spotted two men in very expensive suits being interviewed by Jack Brickhouse. They were still very dry. I crept up behind them, and just as they were about to answer a question, I poured champagne over their heads. As I started to rub it in, I noticed the top part of one man's hair was moving around. By this time, I realized I'd picked out two of the Tribune Company's top executives, one being Stan Cooke. I don't think they cared because the $22 million investment they had made in the Cubs in 1981 had just increased into the hundreds of millions.

Everybody had contributed, including me; I led the league in ground ball outs. Billy Connors had made all the difference. He had faith in me, supported me when I needed it, and kicked me in the butt when I needed that, too. We had an outstanding combination of youth and experience, power and speed. Knowing we'd score runs most of the time allowed me to mature as a pitcher, and with that knowledge and the deep grass of Wrigley's infield, I was happy to induce ground ball after ground ball.

We had done it, together, and more than that, we knew we were good enough to go all the way. Man for man, we matched up well with San Diego, but right from the beginning, things weren't right with the 1984 NL Championship Series. That season a lot of people thought because Wrigley Field was still without lights the TV network wanted the climactic games on in the evening, so we'd only have two games at home instead of the three fans thought we should have had. This wasn't true. Since 1970, the East Division winner had hosted the first two games in every even numbered year and the last three games every odd numbered year. The West Division winner hosted the first two games in every odd numbered year and the last three in even numbered year. When we won the East in 1984, it was our turn to host the first two games and play the last three on the road.

As expected, Frey picked Sut to pitch the opener. Sut was dying to show what he could do. The Dodgers dropped him from their playoff roster before the NLCS in 1981, and Sut, humiliated then, had itched ever since to show Tommy Lasorda what a mistake that had been. The night before Game 1 against the Padres he was so nervous about wanting to play well that he couldn't sleep. He had dreams about the Padres starter, Eric Show, hitting a homer off him and the rest of the Padres doing the same. Instead, it was Sut who did the damage. He went seven innings and gave up just two hits, plus he belted a homer in the third inning.

Sarge knew how to win. He had played on a couple of also-ran Giants and Braves teams early in his career, then played on the Phillies championship team in 1980. He knew what we had to do to win. This was his time to shine. In the first inning, he took Show to a 3-1 count, then lined one into the bleachers. Then in the fifth, he cranked a three-run shot. We scored six runs in that inning, went on to win, 13-0, and were feeling good about ourselves.

Game 2 was my start, but it almost wasn't. Frey's heart fluttered whenever he thought about the issue of whether to start me in one of the most important games in team history. But he followed his gut — and Billy's advice. As usual that year, his gut was right. I was ready. My family life was great at home, and I was always happy because Sandy and I had a most treasured little girl. I wanted to make everyone proud of me and tell that I was a Major League pitcher who could beat the best.

My game I remember well. Before the first pitch, I looked at

Larry Bowa and said, "Are you ready to dance?" Then I just pitched my guts out. My sinker was working that day, and the grounders came, and came, and came. We scored a run in the first when Dernier made a great play, going from first to third on a Ryno grounder. He scored on a Sarge grounder. In the third, Cey doubled in another run, then scored on a sacrifice fly to make it, 3-0. The Padres touched me for a run in the fourth on a Kevin McReynolds sacrifice fly. They scored once again in the sixth on a Steve Garvey RBI single. They took me out with one down in the ninth. I went eight and a third innings, given up two runs and five hits. Of my 25 outs, 17 came on grounders. Lee Smith came in and mopped up a 4-2 win.

Things looked good. In the 15 years of National League play-off series, no team had come back from two straight losses to win. Milwaukee had been the only American League team to do it, in 1982. After Game 2, Frey played it close to the vest. "Strange things can happen," he said. "The talk is that the Cubs are getting all the breaks and the Padres are not, but anything can happen and the direction can change." That was for sure.

Laid-back southern California fans were bonding together and rah-rahing like sixth-grade cheerleaders. *Chicago Tribune* columnist Mike Royko had written an article about the San Diego fans, calling them quiche-eating, Zinfandel-sipping, bored people who never stay past the sixth inning. I went into a car rental place and a restaurant, and both had that article pasted on the wall for everyone to see. As if we needed anything else against us, this rallied them to show up at the airport to greet the Padres after they lost the first two games in Chicago. That column was like a kiss of death for us. In sports, it's best to let your enemy sleep because, if you wake them up, they might catch a few breaks and whip your behind.

Those thoughts weren't on my mind and my family's mind after Game 2. The last time the Cubs were in the World Series, 1945, my father went 1-1 for the Detroit Tigers, who won the series, 4-3. So 1984 was unusual because we won our division, and so did Detroit. Not surprisingly, with a 2-0 lead, my family and the media were ready to head East to Detroit to complete our circle of history because 39 years after Dizzy Trout beat the Cubs in their last World Series, his son would be visiting Detroit as a pitcher for the Cubs to return the favor. This would cause a huge celebration and a remarkable human-interest story for baseball. Detroit had already won the American League pennant, and we hoped to close out our series and set up my storybook match-up.

Friday, Saturday, and Sunday evenings Channel 5 in Chicago brought reporters and TV crews to my mother's house. They came to cover my family's reactions to the series in San Diego because my father had beaten the Cubs in the 1945 World Series and I was now pitching for the Cubs who seemed destined for the 1984 World Series and face the Detroit Tigers again. This was a real baseball story that Channel 5 and NBC didn't want to miss.

Friday night Carol Marin, news anchor for Channel 5, came to the house. (She later moved to the CBS station in Chicago because Channel 5 was broadcasting "The Jerry Springer Show" and she didn't want to work for a station that would air such a tasteless program.) Carol made a good impression on the family. They remember her covering up the smaller children with blankets when they fell asleep. She also told five-year-old Brian, my sister Laura's son, "Now, Honey, when we go on the air to start taping, please make sure your finger is not up your nose." My family really loved Carol because she was so very sweet and loving to them. Aunt Rosie liked her so much that when Carol adopted another child she sent her a Cubs outfit for the baby.

We lost that game, which made an easy exit for the TV crew.

Saturday, Debra Norvill came to the house for Channel 5. She was a little uptight when she met the family. My brother John was smitten with her from the start. Wherever she went in the house, John followed. Debra and my sisters were sitting in the kitchen talking, and John came in and sat down with them to get into the conversation. That's when Debra got up to leave. I don't think John saw any bit of the game. I bet Debra was really hoping it would be a quick game because John was watching her instead of the TV.

Once again another easy exit, but people were getting very nervous because the series was knotted at two games apiece.

Sunday the TV crew arrived in the middle of the game. Tensions were so high in the house that family members hardly knew the camera crew was even there. The crew, however, did videotape the faces of my heart-broken family as the final out was made. All the rubbing of the Buddha's belly that Aunt Rosie brought over for good luck just wasn't enough.

Game 3 was in San Diego, and Dennis Eckersley got the start. We jumped right out on top in the second inning when Moreland doubled and Cey singled to drive him in for a 1-0 lead. Then in the fifth, the Padres hit Eck hard. Old, hobble-kneed Garry Templeton drove in a couple of runs with a double, then he scored on a single for a 3-1 lead. Eck didn't make it out of the sixth, when we gave up four more runs. The final was 7-1, and to be honest, it was no problem. We were still up, 2-1, in the series.

Then the surprise announcement came that Scott Sanderson would pitch Game 4. I was hoping we'd come back with Rick Sutcliffe. But Frey, I think, wanted to keep Sutcliffe to open up the World Series in Detroit, so he was trying to save him. A very reliable source on the team heard Frey say, "There's no way we'll lose Saturday and Sunday, so I'll pitch Sanderson on Saturday." I figured he didn't want me to open up in Detroit. He was banking on a Saturday night victory. I believe Sutcliffe went to management and said, "If you want to re-sign me, then I want to open the World Series in Detroit." I'm just speculating, but that's what I believe. Today, Jim Frey is still waiting for Sut to open up in Detroit.

Not starting Sut proved to be one of the great blunders in Cubs history. Sanderson was a good pitcher, but in a short series like the '84 format, we should have gone with the best we had, and the best we had were Sutcliffe, Eckersley, and me. The best hitter the Padres had was Steve Garvey, and he won Game 4 for them. In the third, he roped a two-run double off Sanderson, and we were down, 2-0. We came back in the fourth for a 3-2 lead on a two-run shot by Jody Davis and a solo homer by Bull Durham. It was tied 3-3 in the seventh when Frey, looking back, made some more questionable moves.

We had a righty reliever, Tim Stoddard, in the game. He walked Bobby Brown with one out. One out after that Frey had Stoddard intentionally walk Tony Gwynn, a left-handed hitter who was the NL batting champ that season. Instead of taking our chances that Gwynn wouldn't double and drive in the go-ahead run, Frey put the tying run on second with Garvey coming up. And Garvey was already 2-for-3, both hits driving in runs with two outs. Garvey lined a single to left, scoring Brown to make it, 4-3, and sending Gwynn to third. Then Jody let a pitch tick off his glove for a passed ball, and Gwynn scored, leaving us down, 5-3. It was no shocker when San Diego manager, Dick Williams, brought in Goose Gossage to close the deal. But we didn't quit. Ryno scratched out a hit on an infield roller and stole second. Moreland singled him in, then Henry Cotto doubled off the wall in center, and we were tied again, 5-5, in the eighth. We could have pulled ahead, but with the bases jammed, Cey grounded out off another reliever, Craig Lefferts. Frey put in big Lee Smith, and he got us through the eighth. In the bottom of the ninth with the score still tied, Gwynn singled off Smith with one out. Then Garvey came up and sent a 1-0 fastball into the outfield seats to win the game. The Padres sprinted off the bench and carried their hero off the field on their shoulders.

That brought us to Black Sunday, October 7, 1984, a day that will live as a never-ending nightmare for all modern-era Cub fans. Even now, I ask the question: Why? And the only answer is, bad decisions and a few terrible breaks, and because, I guess, we were the Cubs. Maybe it was destiny — again. It was almost as if something or someone out of our control was orchestrating the series, taking us on a roller coaster ride that started out gloriously and ended with brakes screeching at rock bottom. It was as if someone dangled the Series in front of us for the entire week, then, right as we reached out to clutch it and make it our own, they took it away, not a trace left behind. But not only that, we shot ourselves in the foot on several occasions, too.

That season we had a team rule that we'd have no family or friends in the clubhouse before the games. It was a good idea, because in California — and Chicago, too — a lot of family and friends and coaches would crash the clubhouse to visit with their players, and it was a distraction when you were trying to focus on winning a ball game.

Before Game 3, as soon as we reached the ballpark in San Diego and settled into the locker room, I noticed Ron Cey's kid there. This kid — who grew up to play in the Twins' organization — was a 9-year-old who thought he was a player on the team. During Game 3 — the first game in San Diego — Bobby Dernier was in the walkway grabbing a cigarette after he had struck out, and the kid says to him, "How can you swing at that pitch?" I couldn't believe what I'd just heard. I thought Bobby was going to kill him, but Bobby just took a big drag on his cigarette. Some-one should have made sure he wasn't in there; however, it wasn't his fault. He turned out to be one of those little annoying dis-tractions that we didn't need at the time, and some of the other guys were saying, "Hey, Cey got his kid in here, why can't I get mine in?"

That kid wasn't the only problem. A couple of celebrities dropped into the clubhouse, stroking the coaches, stroking the players, and nobody in a position of power said anything or tried to put a stop to it. There were almost fights in the clubhouse. There was an actor who lived out there who did favors for the team every once in a while, and during batting practice before one of the games, this not-so-famous actor was in the outfield, shagging fly balls and almost colliding with players. His presence was great for a laugh and for the media, but at one point in the clubhouse I thought Hebner would punch him out.

Moments like these gave me a queasy feeling about where the series was headed. The entire experience will never be forgotten. People will say, "You should have been able to work through that stuff." But it destroys your concentration, throws your psyche out of whack, and creates a genuinely bad karma. When we finally reached Game 5, we could feel the pressure building on us.

In the first inning, Bull started us off by going deep on Eric Show for a two-run homer. Sut was throwing well, as usual, and he went into the bottom of the seventh with a 3-2 lead.

Sut walked Carmelo Martinez on four pitches to start the bottom of the inning. But that was the least of our troubles. Templeton sacrificed him to second. Then stuff just got plain weird. Before the inning, somebody spilled about half the cooler of Gatorade on Durham's glove, just soaking it. He didn't bother to get a new one. Tim Flannery came up and hit a nine-hop-or-so grounder to Durham at first. Leon went down on one knee, like a goalie, to stop the ball, but it went right under his glove and into right field. "You know it's going to come up somewhere," he said after the game. "But it just stayed flat all the way through. I can see it big as day." Maybe it was the sticky glove. Maybe it wasn't. We'll never know. It was only Bull's sixth error of the season. As players, nobody holds that against Leon, and I hope the fans don't either.

The game was tied, 3-3. The 58,000 people in the stands screamed wildly, and their ride was just beginning. Alan Wiggins blooped a sorry single, then Gwynn came up and hit a skidding grounder to Sandberg, and right as the ball reached him, it struck a pebble or a rock or an indentation in the dirt, and rocketed right over Ryno's shoulder into the outfield. It almost hit him square in the face, that's how unexpected it was. Ryno was there; the ball was hit hard, but he was ready to turn the double play and take us out of the inning. The hit was scored a double — rightly so. Flannery and Wiggins scored the go-ahead runs, then Garvey came to bat and singled — what a surprise. Frey went to the mound and lifted Sut and brought me in. "He was pitching a four-hitter," Frey said after the game. "They weren't exactly beating on the ball. I thought he was still throwing the ball well."

And that was it. I pitched two-thirds of an inning of relief, and about all I remember is, I struck out a hitter and made Graig Nettles ground out. Some guys sat in the dugout and watched the Padres and their 58,000 new friends go nuts at our expense. Other guys went to the clubhouse and just sat, staring blindly at nothing, the way you do when you've lost a loved one. Some guys did both. Ryno sought out the solace of the trainer's room and didn't say much to anyone until we left for the airport. Frey walked around the clubhouse slowly and shook everyone's hand, not saying a word. There really wasn't much to say. I remember the bus ride home and how it seemed like it was happening but not really happening. Then it all sunk in. We blew it. Our chance was gone. Yes, our luck was awful, but we also had ourselves to blame. All the distractions we allowed caused friction among the guys and violated the rules that we had all agreed to live under to prevent exactly what we allowed. To this day, I'm still upset with Frey for not having the guts to tell Cey, "The kid's got to go," or to keep the actor out of the clubhouse. The coaches should have said something to keep the team focused.

Maybe I'm one of the few players who still holds onto some of those feelings of shame about what could have been. But in all honesty, I feel I lost more in those three games than anybody could have lost. For me, a Tigers-Cubs World Series and pitching for the Cubs in Tiger Stadium would have been an experience to which you could never attach a price tag. It was about a connection with my dad that, now, I can never have.

That whole experience was so devastating, so oppressing emotionally. Anyone from that team walking around has a huge hole in his heart from that experience. They have to. That series was the opportunity of a lifetime, gone by. It was amazing, and it blows my mind still. We were the better team, and we lost.

* * *

The next task: the reconstruction. As the front office examined the rubble, five of our pitchers were free agents: Eckersley, Sutcliffe, Tim Stoddard, Rick Reuschel, and me. One of the best breaks of my career — having my best season in the last year of my contract — was largely attributable to Billy Connors. He had put his faith in me, and I'd responded. 13 wins were my best. I led the Cubs in games started with 31 and innings pitched with 190. I had six complete games, including two shutouts. I had walked 59 and struck out 80. I led the league in groundball outs thanks to the long grass of Wrigley Field. I had become a pitcher.

In early December, Eck re-signed with the Cubs. Then it was

my turn. I think the Cubs realized they had invested so much time and energy in helping me develop that their best move was to bring me back for the dividend. They had competition. All of 17 clubs contacted my agents, Randy and Alan Hendricks, and said they were interested in me, including the Braves and Yankees. When it came down to it, though, Chicago was the best and only choice. We were settled in suburban Crete, I was playing in front of friends and family, and the Cubs put down money comparable to the best that any of the other clubs were offering.

The Hendricks brothers and the Cubs were at a hotel doing the final negotiations when Charlie Fox called room service and ordered stone crabs for dinner. With buttered fingers, they used a blackboard to hammer out the final contract. The numbers were five years for a total of $4.5 million. Today $4.5 million won't buy you an all-star for even one season. In 1985, though, that was market value, and I was happy. Eventually, Sut signed, too. Stoddard left, and Reuschel was let go. We headed into '85 with one of the best pitching staffs in baseball, and I was determined to have another good year.

I'd had a terrible spring training, when everything I threw was up in the strike zone and hit. When we were in Denver on our way back from spring training, Billy told me I was rushing my hands. They were moving the same time as my legs were. He hadn't told me earlier because he wanted to see if I could figure it out. As soon as I straightened out my mechanics, I was back to my old self. My first start in '85 came on April 11, a Thursday. I stuffed the Pirates, 4-1, giving up just three singles. I threw 101 pitches and got 20 outs on grounders. We were 2-0 and on our way. After the game, I announced I'd donate $300 to the World Hunger Fund for each of my victories. The writers in Chicago had in the paper that "Trout did everything for the Cubs Thursday but solve world hunger, and now he's trying to do that, too." This all started with me seeing a woman named Belle Whaley on "The 700 Club." On December 22, 1984, I had gone to Belle's homeless shelter on the West Side of Chicago and given her a check for $5,000. I gave her the money without saying five words, and she said, "Oh my God! A real live Santa Claus!" (I know something about being Santa Claus because after my first pro season in 1977 I worked at Sears in Calumet City. They said they like me because I was the first Santa they'd had who didn't have alcohol on his breath.) Belle said, "Who are you?"

I replied, "That's irrelevant."

She said, "You have to tell me who you are. I won't be able to sleep otherwise." In the excitement, she didn't look at the check to see I was Steve Trout. She wanted to know more about the person who had given this gift, so I told her. We became very good friends. Over the next year, I was a frequent visitor, helping her feed the homeless in the shelter.

Early in the season, the homeless weren't the only ones who needed help. The Cubs did, too. The injuries came in droves. Dernier went on the DL. Scott Sanderson's back sidelined him. Sarge pulled a muscle in his leg and went on the DL. Sutcliffe pulled his groin running to first, and later hurt his shoulder and went on the DL. Eckersley went down. By the time the All-Star break came, our starting rotation was me, Ray Fontenot, Larry Gura, Dick Ruthven, and a gimpy Sanderson. We were 43-38 halfway through the season, and that 43rd win came on July 9, when I gutted out seven innings and we beat the Padres, 7-3. After that one, my elbow started to hurt. I went on the DL. The season just went on and on like that, one mishap after another, and we finished the year 77-84, 23½ games out of first. I had done what I could to hold the pitching staff together, closing with a 9-7 mark with three complete games and a 3.39 ERA.

The next year was more of the same. We just could not re-capture our health or the magic. Frey was fired, and we finished the season with Gene Michael as our skipper, going 70-90 and finishing 37 games back.

* * *

The Cubs weren't the only ones having trouble. Sandy and I were growing apart, too, which some people might have seen as odd, given the warm relationship between Sandy and my family. In particular, Sandy and my mother were close, in part because they shared a birthday. Sandy respected Mom very, very much. Mom knew that, and with that came a bond that grew. She was like a second mother to Sandy, and my mother had a lot to do with the closeness and love that Sandy and I still have.

But that closeness couldn't save our marriage. We had started drifting apart around 1981, three years after we were married. Taytum's birth strengthened what we had, but it was only a temporary fix. I was living a ballplayer's life on the road all the time. Through the years, I had enjoyed the perks of being a Major Leaguer: the great food and fancy hotels with girls in every town to test your faithfulness. Montreal was always the players' best city for having women. Mostly, they were dancers from Ché Pere, a strip bar two blocks from the hotel. I saw teammates get on their hands and knees towards the end of the night and bark like dogs. This was where you'd leave with a dancer, especially after barking like a dog. Normally, on the way home, you'd know who was cheating on their wife as they'd load up on the duty-free items to give to their loved ones. I called these guilt presents.

Even with Taytum to keep us together, issues kept resurfacing that pulled us apart.

We had a bad year in 1986, and that was when I felt we should separate. We were at Cafe L'Europa in Sarasota that year when I told her that maybe there was somebody better for her, somebody who could live a normal life and give her what she was looking for. She agreed. I didn't want to deprive her of what she might want. I realized I didn't want to have a big family, maybe because I was from one. It was not another woman, not another guy who came between us. It was two people knowing what was best for each other. Even today, we are good friends. I occasionally watch her two boys that she's had with her husband, and I know that part of my relationship with Taytum is a direct result of Sandy's love for me and my family.

Someday I'd like to write a book on how to make a divorce work so you don't lose your child in the event. I think I can offer good advice for couples going through a divorce on how to make it work so they don't lose their respect for each other and the love for their children. That, I feel, was one of the most important and intelligent moves I've made in my life — making the divorce, a potentially devastating situation, into something we could all live with in a positive way. I knew what I needed to get out of it — a relationship with my daughter. So I gave and gave and gave. I gave her the house, the furnishings, the antiques. I gave her the French table that seats 12 people, and the Ethan Allen furniture worth $40,000. One time, I came off a road trip, and I realized we had an addition in one of the corners of the living room. "While you were gone, I thought that space should be filled up," she said. So she bought a mini-grand piano, for $12,000. I gave her that, too, with lessons thrown in, of course.

I only wanted a Chinese lamp and a normal relationship with my daughter that my wife would support. I needed her to be supportive because I was doing everything I could to make it work out for her. It was my way of saying, "Don't fight me over this." All the stuff I gave her, the piano and furniture and who knows what else. It's only stuff. It doesn't breathe, but it was worth millions to me because it gave me the riches of my relationship with Taytum. Couples that are divorcing should see the bigger picture and do everything they can to remember what put them together in the first place, and let that remain in their hearts.

It's hard, getting married at 20 or 21 years old. At that age, what do you really know? Heck, that's how old Taytum will be in four or five years. Still, I'm so happy we did get married and had the years together. Still, the pain of a divorce can cause dramatic changes in your actions and turn you temporarily into a person much different than the one you know.

One 1986 incident in particular is not a pleasant memory. On our way home from downtown after a birthday party, Sandy was driving us home in my Mercedes. On the way home, I got angry about the communication we were having, so I punched the window of the Benz and it cracked. When we got home, I yelled at one of my brothers and fought two of them, biting one. All I remember after that was waking up the next morning and seeing my mother sitting on the bed. She looked at my broken finger and my bloody hand and said, "You need to get help."

I did need help. Mom always said things like, "We are not faucets to be turned on and off," and, "No man is an island." We aren't machines. These are components of our character that determine who we are. Steve Stone, the former Cubs broadcaster on WGN, told me one time that he had personal problems all the time. But he said that when he got up on that hill, on the dirt area of the mound, he was able to concentrate and put all of his troubles out of his mind. He was that faucet, able to turn on and off at will. Steve was able to do everything right, just ask him. He is a very insightful announcer who understands the game very well; however, he has an egotistical side to him that borders on narcissism.

It was just harder for me, plain and simple. I often carried my personal problems and thoughts onto the mound. That's probably why I was a .500 pitcher. Half the time I was happy, and half the time I was struggling with the game, with marriage, with friends, and with whatever else everyone struggles with — only my job was one out of every four days and with the whole world watching.

So I took my mother's advice and called Rick Spattafora, a licensed psychologist actually hired by the Cubs. Dr. Spattafora became a very important person to me. I told him about a lot of problems I was having in life and in baseball, and one was being able to see things through to their completion. I had always had trouble being an effective pitcher after the fourth or fifth inning. By seeing him, I thought maybe I could help my baseball and private life. We talked for about six or seven visits, and on the seventh visit he said, "I think I see a trend here."

One story I told him was about a toy I had put together for Taytum, a car she could ride. Like any father would, I unfolded the directions and followed them, sometimes becoming frustrated but putting great care into the fact that this would be a car that I had assembled for my own daughter. On Christmas, Taytum jumped into the car, excitedly hit the throttle and the car went — backward. I don't even think the car was meant to go backward. Even with all my care, I had not finished the job correctly. I thought about how that was a metaphor for my life at that time.

We talked about my dad. When he died, I was in eighth grade, and how after it happened I put on his long tweed coat and oversized hat and went out and looked for a job, and how that meant I was wrestling with the pressure of the standards Dad had set. I also told Dr. Spattafora that I don't like novels or make believe. Fiction is not my style. I like books about philosophy and about the human mind. Sometimes I'd read a page in one of these books, think about it for days, yet never finish the book.

With my marriage ending after eight years, Dr. Spattafora thought I saw myself as someone who expected himself to fail after accomplishing half of my goal. He said that I had no closure in my life, and that it was something I had come to expect of myself, whether it was on the mound or off it. It made sense. My father died halfway through my childhood. My marriage was failing after eight years. When I read books, I read them halfway through. And after five or six innings, I was often done pitching.

After hearing this, it helped me see it and fix it. Finally, it had hit me that maybe subconsciously I had programmed myself to fail, or at least to struggle in the middle of whatever I was working on.

* * *

So in 1987, with Gene Michael still our manager, I was determined to become a complete pitcher, determined to be a "finisher." When I went to spring training, I was pitching very well. Even in spring training I was pitching six or seven innings, and my mindset was such that I was pushing myself further than I ever had before. The sessions with Dr. Spattafora were paying off.

The season started, and I was fulfilling my goal. I was finishing games, I had a new house in South Holland, and I was adjusting to life away from our house in Crete. I was throwing some of the best baseball in the National League and leading the Cubs rotation.

I suffered a deep thigh bruise diving back to first base during a nationally televised game versus San Diego and went on the DL May 2. A month later I came back against the Phillies and beat them, going eight and two-thirds in the process. We were 34-29 after that game, in second place, and only six behind the division-leading Cardinals. But we had too many DL troubles to contend seriously. Our shortstop, Shawon Dunston, went on the DL with a broken hand the same day I beat Philadelphia. Ryno tore up his ankle and went on the DL. With the middle of our infield on the shelf, we couldn't keep up. We were 47-41 at the All-Star Break, but the Cardinals tore it up, and suddenly we were in fourth and 10 games back.

Seeing that their payroll was large and their chances of winning were small, the Cubs decided to start unloading players. In a few months, they unloaded Eck, Cey, and Sarge.

I was next. On the Sunday leading into the All-Star Break, they threw in the towel officially, sending me to the Yankees for three players: Bob Tewksbury, 26, Rich Scheid, 22, and Dean Wilkins, 21. Dallas didn't tell Gene about it before it happened and with good reason. Gene was miffed. First, because he wasn't consulted; and second, because the Cubs were throwing in the towel. I was coming off two straight shutouts and my market value was never higher. That's what it came down to — money. Being seven games back at the time of the trade and with little chance of winning the division, Dallas was under instructions to unload payroll and make room for two new starters coming into their own; Jamie Moyer and a fellow named Greg Maddux. John Cox called me into the locker room in the eighth inning of Sunday's game to tell me about the deal. I went into a bathroom, locked myself in a stall, and cried.

My life had come to a halt. Even though Sandy and I agreed to separate, I had planned to take Taytum to a resort in Wisconsin Dells for a few days during the break. The trade canceled all that. The writers contacted me at home to find out my reaction to the trade, and I could only tell them I couldn't talk about it now. I wasn't trying to be difficult. I just couldn't talk about it. It was so sudden, so unexpected that I didn't know what to feel, other than shock. The day of the All-Star Game, Tuesday, July 14, I held a press conference on my mom's front lawn in South Holland.

I'd never pitch in Wrigley again, but that would be the least of my concerns.

	1	2	3	4	5	6	7	8	9	R	H	E
Visitor	0	0	0	1	0	1						
Home	1	0	2	1	0	0						

Losing Control

People in Chicago think New Yorkers are arrogant, fast-paced, and ready to trample over you if you move too slowly or make the wrong turn.

The people in Chicago are right.

But there is something about "The Big Apple" that is electric and gives you the feeling that right now, right here, you are in the place that matters most. There's a mythology that is like no other. Even when I was with the White Sox, I loved pitching in Yankee Stadium. There is no other place a pitcher would rather do well. Yankee Stadium has that mystique, that history about it that makes it unlike any other park. When you're playing in "The Big Apple," you can feel the world's breath on your neck and its eyes watching your every move. That sense that you're on stage makes you want to be at your best every time you take the mound. I loved New York as much as I hated it.

If you were playing at Yankee Stadium, you learned something really fast: Always wear a protective hat. It could be the water, or it could be the program of intensive training passed through the generations, or maybe they're hoping a scout will notice and ask them to take the mound for the bottom of the ninth. But for some reason, New York fans are among the world's best at hurling objects at people. In Boston, they spit better.

I have been hit by Eveready batteries, beer cups — full and empty — chicken bones, and hot dogs. I have been called every name in the book, mostly by the right field area at Yankee Stadium and Fenway Park, where — as in many other parks — the right field fans seem to be a little more hostile than the rest of the park. Then there are occasions where these same fans make some wonderful gesture of kindness to help somebody out. One time, a young fan took a line drive straight on, and I remember the concern and help that all the fans gave that little boy.

You could say New York contains the worst and best of what

fans can be. Their intensity is what makes them some of the best baseball fans around. But I would see mostly the worst, and sadly, I couldn't do much about it.

* * *

The Yankees were right in the heat of the pennant race in 1987, and they needed pitching. To them and anyone who knows baseball, trading for me made sense, especially considering the roll I was on in my final weeks with the Cubs. A hard-throwing left-hander with a good sinker would be the perfect way to keep a lid on those other power-hitting AL East teams. On paper, the Yankees had outsmarted their competition. In reality, they had acquired a pitcher who was about to endure one of the most demoralizing stretches of his life. The next few months changed the whole direction of that pennant race, the Yankees' season, and my baseball career.

The fateful moment took place in Comiskey Park, in my second start for the Yankees. The place where it all began was also the place where it would start to end.

Standing there before the game in a Yankees uniform felt strange to me. After all those years as a Chicago pitcher, there I was in pinstripes. I sensed a haze and a touch of vertigo when I took the mound in the second inning and prepared to throw my warm-up pitches. I wound up, but the pitch got away from me and sailed to the backstop. The umpire, Ken Kaiser, looked at me as if to say, "Damn! You almost hit me!" The next warmup pitch hit the dirt, and Rick Cerone, our catcher, shot a puzzled look at me.

When the batter stepped in, my first live pitch went into the dirt. My response was fear — pure fear of having no idea where the next pitch would go. My arm felt like it had lost its looseness, its ability to relax and throw a baseball. It felt tight, as if I had just lifted weights. Taking that baseball and pinpointing it to the corner of the plate seemed an impossibility to me. I lasted four innings that day with one wild pitch that went to the screen.

The troubles were just beginning. I started thinking all the time about throwing wild pitches in games. It was all I could think of. I kept visualizing the negative. Pitching became a battle. Just to feel good about pitching when I wasn't pitching was a struggle. My fears got the best of me. I had dreams about wild-pitching. It was with me 24 hours a day.

That summer of 1987 would become the "Endless Summer" for me. I couldn't throw the ball the way I wanted. My left arm tightened into a hard mass of muscle every time I picked up a baseball, and thoughts of throwing it into the dirt or over the umpire's head replaced thoughts of painting the corners. Playing pepper or even catch became an ordeal. Cerone, our starting catcher, ripped me in the clubhouse, asking how they could have traded for this head case.

On July 29, the night before my birthday, I didn't sleep. I was starting the next day against the Royals in New York; and I was having anxiety about where the ball could go, how my arm would feel, and how the whole pattern could repeat itself again. Then I began to pray.

Praying has always been important to me. Some people pray only when they are in need, and I can never understand that. How can you pray when times are tough and never when life is going well? That's why I pray and believe in prayer, and I believe in trusting your spiritual sense, regardless of what your situation is. Now I pray to thank God for everything. I made a commitment to prayer. It's very hypocritical to ask God for help when you are in need, and not do it when you are sailing along just fine. It's not what the church can do for me every Sunday; it's what my relationship is to God.

The following day, my birthday, Mark Salas was catching and not Cerone, and I actually pitched well. I threw six shutout innings with six strikeouts. Lou Piniella, our manager, came up to me in the dugout after the sixth and said, "Nice job. Do you want to keep going?"

I looked at him and said, "No, I've had enough." I ended up not getting the win, but the team did.

After the game, George Steinbrenner had a two-foot-tall bottle of champagne sent to my locker, but I felt bad. I never would have taken myself out when I was pitching for the Cubs or Sox. But in my current state, I just wanted to get a game under my belt. I felt really bad about that, like I had wimped out or something.

It reminded me of a feeling I had once when I was with the Cubs and playing the Giants. Dan Gladden took out Sandberg real hard at second base on a double play. It was my duty to give Gladden "the message" with a ball at his head, but instead I missed. Then I just pitched to him instead of nailing him to retaliate for Ryno. My teammates were upset with me for not carrying through with my part, and you also lose respect for yourself. You must protect your hitters under all circumstances.

The Yankees eventually gave up on me as a starter and sent me to the bullpen. The coaches thought removing the anxiety of being a starter would put me on a more instinctual path and that I wouldn't have time to think about all that could go wrong. But my next two appearances were nightmares: seven walks in three and two-thirds innings, four wild pitches.

And then, in August, in Tiger Stadium, with the pennant race heating up and the eyes of New York upon me, the wheels fell off in a relief appearance few will ever forget. I was praying not to go into the game, but the phone rang. Even my warm-up pitches were a battle of nerves.

When I took the mound in the game, I threw 11 pitches, and none of them seemed to find their way to Cerone. Baseballs missed home plate, bounced into the dirt, caromed off the screen. Short, wide — you name it. I threw it anywhere out of the strike zone. And with every pitch the pressure built like a dam in my head about what would, or could, happen on the next pitch.

Eventually, Piniella came out to the mound because I was suffering so badly. The damage was done. No innings, one hit, two runs, two walks. Two wild pitches. Cerone was exhausted when it was over and told the media after the game that it was the longest and worst inning of his career, too. That got back to me, and it was like putting salt into a terrible wound. I had always realized the importance of a pitcher-catcher synergy, but Cerone was not a catcher who had sense enough to see the team picture. He was using me as his joke, and I lost all respect for him.

The next pitcher, Al Holland, didn't get to warm up because my mental injury wasn't considered the same as a physical one. On his third pitch, his arm broke. I was sitting in the dugout watching them tend to this teammate in agony. Al wouldn't pitch in the Major Leagues again. I felt so ashamed of myself. I felt responsible for Al's injury. All I had to do was pitch one inning and give him time to loosen up. But I couldn't, and Al had no time to prepare. It hurts me today, even thinking about it.

After the inning, I looked at my hand and saw bruises. During it all when they were looking at Al and taking him away, I was banging my hand on the wood bench at Tiger Stadium.

From then on, the team and front office treated me like a leper, although there were a few great guys — Don Mattingly, Rickey Henderson, Dave Winfield, Dave Righetti among them — who tried to be supportive. Thinking of them makes me think about how wonderful it could have been.

After my bad outing in Detroit, Piniella called me into his office after batting practice the next day, and after stepping over some dirty underwear and jock straps, I sat down. He had Billy Connors on the phone, and because Billy was with the Seattle Mariners at the time, the call was a surprise. Lou probably thought he could make something happen like in the movie, "The Manchurian Candidate," where Billy says a couple of secret, hypnotic words and all of a sudden I snap out of it. But I felt the call to Billy was desperation at best.

The Yankees did try a couple of other quick fixes. They suggested Valium, or whatever drug could defuse my anxiety. They hired a special pitching coach to come into Kansas City and watch me throw in the bullpen. I threw well, and he said, "All you have to do is throw like that." Pitching in the bullpen is one thing, but pitching in a game is another. Once we walked to the bullpen and the national anthem was sung, I then secretly wished I wouldn't get into the game.

The media and the fans in New York couldn't understand what had happened any better than I could. The Yankee brass wanted to know, too, so they put a private eye on me.

At the time, I was living in Tenafly, New Jersey. One day I came out of my house and noticed a guy sitting in his car down the street facing me. I got in my car and drove by him. He immediately made a U-turn and started following me. I didn't know what to think. I didn't know this guy or what he wanted, so I took a roundabout route to Yankee Stadium, running red lights and stop signs along the way and almost killing myself. I figured he was either tailing me or he had something to do with a death threat I'd received recently. As soon as I got to the ball park, I stomped through the stadium and ran up to Steinbrenner's office, but he wasn't in. But Woody Woodward, the assistant GM (who just retired from the Seattle Mariners), was, and I pleaded with him to do one of two things: if it was a psycho fan on my tail, have somebody take care of it; and if it was a tail from the team, pull him off. I was scared stiff. Immediately after that, it stopped.

Why did they tail me? They probably thought I was hanging out in crack houses or something like that. But it was all in my head. All you need to do is just concentrate and throw the ball over the plate, right? But anyone who understands the human mind will tell you, it doesn't work that way. The response is just like when someone says not to think about pink elephants. What do you do? You think about pink elephants. It was the same for me. The more someone told me, "Don't think about it," the more I would think about it.

Everyone did what they could to help. My brother Ross, who was a high school baseball coach and English teacher in south suburban Chicago, tried to put it as simply as possible. "Steve," he said, "just let them hit the freaking ball!" And it was like a light went on: Yeah! That's it! Let them hit the ball! I had never thought of the game quite like that, and that helped me — some.

Pitchers are taught not to let guys hit the ball, but when you think about it, you have eight players behind you, and most of the time hitters will get themselves out. Bob Gibson, the great Cardinals pitcher of the 1960s, never really started to pitch until somebody got on base. He was smart. He was conserving his strength.

Ross's advice didn't do the trick, though. My hand still clutched the baseball like a locking wrench. The backstop behind the catcher still seemed like it was a million miles away. My arm tightened into a knot.

When you're struggling, everybody tries to help. People tried reverse psychology — telling me to throw the ball away from the catcher. So many people telling me so many different things. Take a Valium before you pitch. Smoke a joint before you pitch. Anything.

Some people wanted me to fail, too. From the day I arrived in New York, Cerone was a complete jackass to me. He never made me feel like I was part of the team and always sent the vibe that he didn't want to talk to me or that he was better than everyone else. And when my world was falling apart, Cerone was more than happy to throw some rock salt on the most open wound he could find. He'd say, "Hey, Trout! The light's on, but nobody's home." That's not the way you want your catcher talking when you're a pitcher. If I'd been an infielder, it wouldn't have mattered so much. I sometimes think it would have been better to hash it out with him, but I know that people like Cerone just hurt themselves in the long run. I even wish I would have done what Ron Guidry said. "If you want to throw up, just go ahead. It'll make you feel better." I believe he was right. I saw the movie, "Any Given Sunday," where the third string quarterback barfed on the sidelines and after his jitters were over, he was throwing bullets. Many athletes have encountered some type of anxiety in the course of their careers.

One of the guys on the team I felt I had a friendship with was the other catcher, Mark Salas. But even he was against me on this. On a road trip to Cleveland, I was about to knock on his door to grab lunch when I overheard him on the phone, telling someone,

"You should see Trout! He's all over the place. He couldn't find home plate with a phone book." I was devastated; I ate by myself.

That episode confirmed to me that people are phony, and finding a good friend would be that much more difficult.

With all this happening, a feeling crept into my mind that I had never had before. I started to fear going to the ballpark. This is the way Mitch Williams must have felt when he was with the Phillies a few years ago. Every day is a nightmare. A sick feeling invaded my stomach every time I walked into the ballpark. It was so tough. Even on my days off, I would go to Yankee Stadium, take a ball, and throw it against the outfield wall, and I would repeat to myself, "I'll get this thing back. I'll get this thing back."

Nothing was right with my pitching again. Eventually, it reached the point where if a right-handed batter came up I had no problem. If a left-hander came up, though, the alarm bells went off. What if I hit him in the head, I thought. I'd throw one over his head, then I couldn't make the adjustment. If I was warming up, throwing to a catcher, and let's say there's a fence behind him, I felt fine. But if I was throwing to a catcher to get my work in on the side and saw the screen way in back of the catcher, my arm tightened up like a short rubber band. A close backstop seemed to have a positive effect on me.

Sliders, I could have thrown them all day to lefties and had no problem. But when I threw a fastball my mind jumped into a state of anguish, a frustration of not feeling like I could cut loose, of fearing where the ball might end up.

During that half-season in New York, rock bottom was so low that some nuts were making threats against my life, which didn't help. Dave Righetti would hold up my death threats and yell out, "Trout got another one." I led the team in that dubious category. I was only mildly concerned about these threats, but subconsciously, I wanted to be put out of my misery.

Recently, Major League Baseball implemented a network of security agents in each big league city to protect their own. I believe this was done in light of the John Rocker incident. These special agents are on call for all players if they need assistance for any off field problems. Each player was given a card with toll free numbers to reach the agents.

This service would have helped me, but I would have needed my own set of bodyguards to escort me in and out of Yankee Stadium due to the way I was pitching and the number of death threats I was receiving.

* * *

About the only good times in New York were the "Beach Parties," the best part of road trips. Guys on the team would roam the hotel, collecting the plants from the lobbies and common area, then they'd put them in the room selected for the party. We'd put on our bathing suits and Hawaiian shirts and fill up a busboy's tray with about 10 gallons of water. Imagine Don Mattingly doing our trademark move, the "head dunk." He'd bounce up and down on the bed, then land on all fours before plunging his head into the water. Then you'd shake your head like a soggy dog and spray water everywhere. Tim Stoddard was my favorite, all 6'8" 275 pounds of him. That was a big splash. The "Beach Parties" were a good idea because it was harmless fun, a chance for guys to blow off steam. And oddly enough, Yankees, usually a team with the most high-priced free agents, managed to find a way to stick together. They didn't go out on the town in cliques; they hung out together. Maybe that's another reason for their success through the years.

One big party we had at the end of the season was paid for by the "kangaroo court" money. The "kangaroo court" is where players are fined for all kinds of mistakes they make during the season. Two players are elected as judges, and once a week you have a team trial. Players were fined for not running out a ball, showing up late, missing a bus, not moving a runner over from second to third with less than one out. One of the most expensive fines was when someone stole another guy's girlfriend on a road trip. That was called "pulling the sheets" and was subject to a $50 fine. Another hefty fine, $25, was when a player had his "dick in the spread" — an infraction when a player didn't cover up his private parts as he leaned over the buffet table during the postgame meal. There were many other fines. The fines would be collected over the course of the season, and one hell of a party would be thrown, usually during the last road trip.

Once in Toronto when I was with the Yankees, Ron Guidry standing at the podium with the microphone in his hand, held up two skewers and said, "The tightest ass award goes to Steve Trout. Hey, Trout. See if you can fit these up your ass." Everyone laughed, even me outwardly, but inside I was hurting.

In order to make the party real festive, we would have guys go through area shopping malls and become baseball "scouts," but we would look for a different kind of talent — the female variety. The party would last all night, and the next day, many bench players would start.

Through my time in New York, the most helpful and patient man in the organization was "The Boss," George Steinbrenner. We met on an elevator after one of my first few days with the team, and he was cordial and pleasant. The intimidating effect he has on lots of people didn't really happen to me. The awe wasn't there for me, maybe because I had grown up around so many baseball people. When Ted Williams, a good friend of my dad, comes to your house when you're a kid, you're not intimidated or impressed by much.

George was genuinely concerned about me. I knew as much, but other people told me, too. He had some horse racing interests, and one day during the '87 season he was at Balmoral Park in suburban Crete, where my house was. At the track, somebody recognized Steinbrenner and went up to him and said, "Hey, George, I guess Trout just isn't doing the job for you guys."

And George said, "Aw, he must be awfully homesick."

The thing was, George didn't know this was my high school coach. He could have used me as a scapegoat for the entire season. After all, he had traded for a guy who was pitching well and whose only wish was to win a pennant, then I fell apart. If I had pitched without any problems — maybe six innings each outing, two or three runs — we would have won the division. I believe that. But on an occasion when he could have ripped me to someone, he didn't, and I respect that.

As far as I was concerned, George was a demanding owner but a decent guy. I don't know if it was that he could relate to what I was going through at that time; he just seemed to understand and wanted to help fix things any way he could. He felt the pain for me. I really believe that. He never pressured me. He wanted me to do good, not for him, but for me. I think the guy's got a huge heart and is a pioneer, an incredible leader.

During my time there, the fans in New York put up banners that said, "George leave town!" and "George must go!" They wouldn't put those banners up now. But that's just the way New Yorkers are. They demand to win, and in Steinbrenner, that's what they have — a winner.

I think what people respect most about him is that everyone knows what he's all about. He doesn't bullshit people. If he's excited for you, he'll say so. If he's pissed, he'll tell you that too. Rarely will he blindside you. I would love to be working for the guy someday because his loyalty is thick.

Most of the players learned not to mess with George, and Piniella was good at knowing how to handle the situation. When George was his strong-willed, outspoken self, Piniella took precautions. My very first week with the Yankees, Piniella called a team-only meeting after batting practice in Detroit. He made everybody sit down and hushed the room real quiet. "All right. George is up to his old tricks again. He's on the warpath. Rickey," he said to Rickey Henderson, "whatever you read in the papers tomorrow, I didn't say that. Don," he said to Mattingly, "whatever you read, I didn't say that either. Winnie," he said to Dave Winfield, "same for you."

As it turned out, all the papers were going to receive the word that certain guys weren't doing the job, and the anonymous quotes were going to come from George, not Piniella. Lou wanted to protect himself.

One game, my best in New York, I actually made it all the way to the seventh inning. I had a shutout going, and there was a routine fly ball hit to Henry Cotto. At a time when I really needed some help, Henry lost the ball in the lights and let it bounce off the heel of his glove. After a walk or something, there was a grounder in the hole at shortstop to Bobby Meacham, who reached the ball but didn't throw anywhere because he didn't think he could beat the runner. Then Juan Beniquez came up and hit a ball that bounced, literally, off the top of the right-field wall and went out for a grand slam. Four runs, we were down 4-0. Another base hit, and Piniella — who hates all pitchers — came out to yank me. He said in all the 25 years he'd had in baseball, he'd never seen an inning like that. I headed down to the locker room. Someone had the Seattle front office confront him about his anger toward pitchers. Many times he has exchanged harsh words while removing a pitcher. I can just see him sitting in an anger management class vowing to be nicer to his staff.

I was in the clubhouse tearing off my uniform when I heard a guy come running into the locker room. I thought it was one of my death threats, but it was only George. He looked into the locker room, saw Claudell Washington, and said, "What the hell are you doing in here?" Claudell said he was DH-ing. Then he saw Gary Ward and asked him the same thing. Gary gave him the same answer. And George said, "Oh, okay." Hopefully by now, somebody has told George that each team is only allowed one DH in a game.

George started looking around some more and I noticed that

Ron Kittle was also in the clubhouse, actually coming out of a stall with his pants half-way down his legs. He scrunched real low to the ground and snuck to the dugout because, if George saw him, he'd be on the "Columbus Shuttle," as we called it.

Then George looked at me and said, "You could have won that ballgame tonight if it weren't for Cotto and Meacham."

I looked at him and said, "George, Bobby made a good play. He was in the hole and had to do something. Yeah, maybe a great throw gets him at first, but he had to go for a play."

"Bullshit!" George said. "Meacham should have made that play to second or first."

I tried to defend Bobby, thinking he could use the support, but it didn't help. Thank goodness, the starting shortstop hurt himself in the game as flight arrangements had already been made to send Bobby on the "Columbus Shuttle."

This was how George worked, and I was seeing it firsthand. If you work for George and he likes you, you have a job for life; that is, unless you're a manager. They just get hired to get fired or get *re-hired* to get *re-fired*. George is a tough businessman who built his businesses into an empire. George isn't a heartless, cut-throat guy like some people make him out to be. It's well known how George helped one of his former pitchers get out of debt by buying his oil investments and writing them off as a loss. He just wants his employees to have the same work ethic he has.

I regret not doing better for him, especially after how he tried to help me. But George couldn't help me. Billy Connors couldn't either. Nobody could.

What happened? That was a question I wrestled with for years. I think it had something to do with the trade, which took me out of my comfort zone and away from everything I knew, at a time when I was finally starting to pull my career together. I had grown up in Chicago; played high school baseball in Chicago; when I was drafted, it was by the Chicago White Sox; when I was traded, it was just across town, to the Chicago Cubs. My family was in Chicago, my ex-wife and daughter lived there, and Chicago was my home. I fought the game. Somehow, we clashed. Maybe the game was too easy for me. I believe when things are easy for you, you have a tendency not to respect it enough. I was physically strong and never experienced a career-ending physical injury. I was instead mentally injured, which in many ways can be worse. Life has its own way of working things out, one way or another. I was often torn between my love for the game and my love for the simple life, the life of being real and at peace. Baseball and I struggled that way. So often in the month of July, I would hit a brick wall and come crashing down; some-times, I'd seriously think about quitting. My wife and I would talk about growing flowers and herbs in the mountains of Montana. This was my burn-out period each year which would last for a couple of weeks; however, it would go away. Those were my "dog days of summer."

I was also torn between my love for baseball and my love for the single life, the life of living peacefully and more in tune with Nature. The game was such a fish bowl existence that I would fight the stardom. I fought the artificiality of it. It was very phony at times. The purity was when I was on the hill and ready to compete.

I went to spring training that year with a sunny outlook on the season. For once, life was stabilizing, on and off the field. Then, they traded me. I was in New York, my stable routine shattered and my emotions scrambled. The move was like another divorce on top of the one I already had, tearing me away from everything I had ever known and cared about. It was like vertigo, a very disorienting feeling that leaves you rudderless and confused. Chicago was my security blanket, and it was ripped out of my hands.

The Yankees had also seen something ripped away from them — the pennant. At season's end, my AL stats read 0-4 with an ERA of 6.60. We finished the season 89-73, a good record, but still nine games behind the division-champ Tigers. The last day, as we were packing up our stuff and leaving the clubhouse, I walked up to Lou and said, "I'm sorry." Steve Trout, the kid with the God-given gun for a left arm, had done something his dad would never have done: He had let his mind get the best of him.

I wasn't the first to suffer what's known as "Steve Blass Syndrome." Our affliction is named for the righty who was the hero of the 1971 World Series for the Pirates against the Orioles. The following year he went 19-8 with a 2.48 ERA. Then, like me, he inexplicably couldn't throw the ball over the plate anymore. He was 3-9 with a 9.85 ERA in 1973. By 1974, he was out of baseball, at age 32. Kevin Saucier, a lefty reliever for the Tigers, had 13 saves and four wins in 1981 before developing Blass Syndrome. He was afraid of hitting batters and was out of the game in 1982 at age 26. A former Sox pitcher, Joe Cowley, threw a no-hitter for them in 1986. After developing Blass Syndrome and going 0-4 for the Phillies in 1987, they sent him to the minors, and he couldn't get the ball over there either, so he left the game. Mark Wohlers was one of the best relievers in the game with the Braves a few years ago. Today, he can't throw the ball over the plate. That look on his face speaks loud and clear to me. I have been tempted to call him or the organization to speak to him. I can feel his pain. When you're going through something like that, it helps to see how others have dealt with it, but you have to come out of it your own way, too.

Baseball people call it "The Thing." It's when you can't throw the ball to your target, or you can't hit a ball right there in the strike zone. "The Thing," or "The Black Hole" as I call it, comes when you least expect it or when you least want it. For me, it was when I became New York Yankees pitcher, when I joined the mythology, the history of this great organization, to be part of the pin-stripes.

Players don't understand this "Thing." They coined "The Thing" because they don't know what causes it, why it's there, or when it will leave. Psychologists suggest it's not just in athletes, but can be found in everyone. Harvey Dortman wrote: "Jerks of the world don't usually have this problem." It usually strikes wonderful guys; sensitive, caring, good people. Guys insensitive to the judgement of others generally don't have this problem. Others who have been affected are Mackey Sasser, Steve Sax, Steve Blass, Chuck Knoblauch, and Rick Ankiel. For Ankiel, it came at it's most unfortunate time, Game 1 of the Division Series versus the Atlanta Braves. Sandy Koufax fought severe control problems that almost ended his career. I witnessed a minor league pitcher for the Pirates who come from the Dodgers in a trade who had a horrible case of "The Thing." Jockeys, golfers, writers, actors, hockey players, and even basketball players have fought this "Thing." It's in all of us.

When I was with the Yankees and living in Tenefly, New Jersey, I started putting the bed in front of the bedroom door as if that would keep "The Thing" out of the room. "The Black Hole" was with me every second of the day. Paranoia even took over. I woke up choking at times, with nothing lodged in my thoughts, simply a feeling of being overwhelmed and dealing with more than I could chew.

I fought "The Thing" for years, even after I was out of base-ball, until my comeback with the Pirates in '97 allowed me to get rid of the nightmare. I thank Cam Bonifay for giving me the chance for one last effort to finish baseball in a better way.

* * *

A day or two after the 1987 season ended Mom and I planned a car trip up the eastern seaboard, a nice chance to see the fall colors. Our plan was to do the bed-and-breakfast circuit through Connecticut, Maine, Boston, and Rhode Island on a 10-day trip. Mom, as usual, felt comfortable at home, and the only way I could ensure she'd be on the plane was to send her a non-refundable plane ticket.

While we were gone, I wanted to leave my Mercedes in the shop to have some body work done, the result of a run-in between my unattended car and a fan at Yankee Stadium while we were away on a road trip. The vandal had broken a window, stolen the Benz logo off the hood ornament, and ransacked the interior. Good security. I guess Mercedes hood ornaments are a status symbol for the youth of the Bronx. Okay, I thought, it's the Bronx and it was lucky they didn't burn the car to the ground. One of the front-office staffers with the Yankees called to tell me that my car had been vandalized. I decided to take the car in for repairs to a recommended Benz dealership in New Jersey, and there some very strange things happened.

The owner of the dealership was an okay guy who said, "I'll let you borrow a dealer Benz for your trip, and when you get back, your car will be tuned up and ready for the trip back to Chicago."

As I picked up the loaner, I entered the service area and over-heard two of the guys in the garage talking about me. "Hey," one guy said, "did you see that Trout guy pitching the other night? That sonofabitch looks like he's on another planet or something. He should quit baseball."

"Yeah, he's a bum," the other guy said. "What a big mistake Steinbrenner made."

They held nothing back, and I had to walk out of the garage and settle down before I went back in and paid for the service. As I stood outside, steaming, I decided jumping over the counter and knocking them over the head with a crowbar wouldn't be the smartest response. I had to be cool. Yes, I wanted to lash out, but I handled it correctly.

I walked back in with a credit card in hand and slapped it down. Both guys stood there, and one picked up the card and walked to the back with it. When my bill came back, I signed it, without one word being exchanged. They knew it was me by then, and there was a heaviness in the air. They knew there was a part of me that wanted a part of them.

Mom and I had a great time, eating lobster sandwiches in Maine, pizza at Pepe's in New Haven, Connecticut — the best pizza in the world. In Boston, we ate oysters at the Union Oyster House. In Rhode Island, we visited the Astor Mansion. What a trip!

We returned to the dealership, but it was closed, except for the general manager who was there to switch cars with me. It was a quick exchange. My mom got into the car, and I did too, except as I opened the door for her, I spotted something peculiar. Drawn on the front right tire was a yellow circle, and upon closer inspection, I looked down and found a bubble in the tire that was the size of a 12-inch softball — about the size my pitches were looking in those days.

I said, "Hey, what's this! You mean in two weeks they didn't fix this mistake?" Then I stopped and thought about it. Maybe it wasn't a mistake. Wouldn't it be convenient for the guys in the shop if that Trout bum who pitches for the Yankees drove home on a dangerous blistered tire? I was pissed off big-time. I drove to a Goodyear tire store and had it taken care of, thinking how lucky I was the guys there didn't know they were putting four fresh ones on for the Yankees pitcher who helped blow the pennant.

I had to try something to set my mind straight again. So in November, I visited Billy Connors for a week in Florida. As it turned out, Billy had some plans of his own. He decided that if he was going to be running up his long-distance bill with calls to New York, he might as well have me on his staff. With his recommendation, the Mariners made the deal, sending the Yankees reliever Lee Guetterman for me and Henry Cotto, who's now a Double -A coach with the Mariners. Billy, in fact, was the one who called me up and told me about the trade. And not long after that, I had the strangest dream.

I was in very rough seas aboard a very large boat, and the waves and the wind were tossing and pitching the boat every which way. This violent weather went on for quite some time, until I found myself in a smaller boat, something like a dinghy, and I was the only one in the boat. Then a huge wave approached on the horizon. As it reached me, the dinghy rode up on the wave like a surfboard. When I reached the top of the wave, I shot off it, blasting skyward like a rocket. The boat landed on a peaceful mountainside. I was surrounded by serene sun and light breezes, with mountain grasses and small spring flowers all around.

The next day I asked my brother Paul what he thought the dream meant, and he told me what a "Mariner" was. Back then, you see, I had no idea a Mariner was a boat person. So it made sense after analyzing the dream.

When I arrived in Seattle and met with the Mariners' sports psychologist, Dr. Bennett, he explained that the dream was affirmation that the storm was New York and the peace was Seattle. The storm was over, and serene time was about to begin. He also said that it was time to return to feeling relaxed on the mound, regain my confidence, and let go of the ball with no fear.

Dr. Bennett was very helpful. He seemed genuinely concerned about me, and of course, he wanted credit if I should come around to my old self. He wanted me to pitch well. But the dream was at least some sort of positive sign that there was sunlight at the end of the darkness.

Seattle was a pleasant experience. There was a good feeling around the clubhouse, around the people, the fans. Strange fans, stranger than anywhere I'd seen. You saw more people sitting by themselves watching a game than anywhere else. It was a very dispersed crowd, very quiet, but a very friendly town, a very warm sort of sleepy town. By 10 o'clock the town rolled up its streets and went to sleep. It was a healthy environment. I enjoyed taking the ferries over to Bainbridge Island and driving around the picturesque towns of Kirkland and Redmond. The home I rented on Mercer Island had a balcony where I could see a beautiful view of the city skyline and the many sailboats. Seattle back then had more boats per capita than cars.

And the players were supportive of each other. They kind of realized we were like "The Dirty Dozen," a makeshift team. Ken Griffey, Jr., was a rookie on that team in '89, and we became friends. I liked the kid a lot, thought a lot of him. Not only did he have a huge amount of talent, he handled himself really well. During his rookie season a guy from the Seattle area made a candy bar for Griffey. He produced a million of them, and they sold out fast and no more were ever made. It was a one-time deal, and I think it was Griffey's first money-making endorsement. Even though Griffey is gone, his candy bar still remains in the freezers of many of his loyal fans.

As for myself, Billy used to say that he could tell what kind of game I was going to have by watching my first throw in the bullpen and my demeanor when I walked out to the mound for my

111

first pitch. If the bill of my cap was pulled off-center, the bullpen was on red alert. If it was straight and pulled down tight over my eyes, he knew it could be a good day.

My failure to regain what I had lost, though, wasn't a function of being spacey or a lack of intensity as much as it was the anxiety of throwing the ball. Billy and I spent the month before spring training working in Florida, and he had me do a drill where he would put me deep at second base and have me field grounders. The idea is that you're just throwing the ball to first base, not making a huge, cerebral deal out of it, and that this was a drill to put me back on the right track.

At spring training that year, the work looked like it would pay off. When the season started, my control was improved and I had earned a spot in the starting rotation.

Then came my debut against Oakland. After retiring the first two batters, I walked one batter. Then another. And another. And another. And another after that. Two runs scored on *very* wild pitches, and with one of them, I was so dumbstruck by what was happening that I just stood there and didn't cover home plate as the runner scored. "He lets the ball defeat him," Billy told the media, trying to explain me.

But by May, I had managed to turn my 54.00 ERA into a 3-2 record and a 6.58, and then a guy on the Tigers hit a shot back at me that sailed just past my left ear. I stuck up my left hand at the last second, purely out of instinct, and the ball smacked it. As the trainer came out to the mound that day to examine my broken finger, one thought ran through my mind: "Thank God I don't have to struggle like this anymore."

Newspaper clippings from Dad's win over the Cubs in the 1945 World Series.

Tony LaRussa and me in our better days. Tony managed me at Double-A Knoxville, and we came to the big leagues at almost the same time.

Me in those funky "throwback" uniforms that Bill Veeck designed for the White Sox back in the 1970s.

I'm #51 looking at Duane Shaffer (now head scouting director for the Chicago White Sox) for some pitching instruction, while Marv Foley (in the batting helmet and now with the Baltimore Orioles coaching staff) and Joe Gates take a breather before the game starts.

My brothers, sisters, Mom, and me in front of our South Holland home, doing a move from "Chorus Line." Mom is fifth from the right. I'm not sure why she wasn't in the center, but I guess it's indicative of a slightly balanced family.

115

My dad with his arm around his skipper and the greatest player of all time, Babe Ruth, in Lakeland during spring training. I don't know the other man in the photo.

This was in the New York newspapers. Dad and Hal Newhouser, left, indicating they were both 20-game winners; Newhouser won 29, and Dad 27. It's still a baseball record: 56 wins by two pitchers on the same team.

Dad and Ted Williams laugh it up at a hunting and fishing lodge. Maybe those cases of beer are half empty . That coat Ted has on is still in the family.

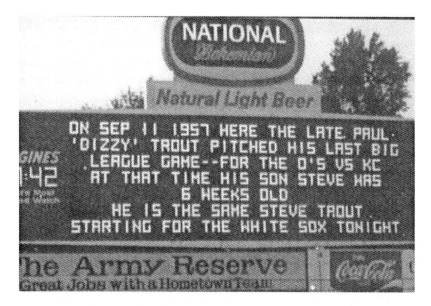

ON SEP 11 1957 HERE THE LATE PAUL
'DIZZY' TROUT PITCHED HIS LAST BIG
LEAGUE GAME--FOR THE O'S VS KC
AT THAT TIME HIS SON STEVE WAS
6 WEEKS OLD
HE IS THE SAME STEVE TROUT
STARTING FOR THE WHITE SOX TONIGHT

A very proud day for me when the Orioles put this on their scoreboard in Baltimore. I only wish I could have seen some of my dad's pitching career.

Father-Son game at Comiskey Park. Eddie Stanky has his arm around me. He later gave me some chewing tobacco. From left to right, Bob, Ross, and John. Dad is still looking for the pitcher in one of his boys.

Who says the Cubs don't have class? Team picture at a Cubs Care fund-raiser. That's me in the middle row, all the way to the right, with my arm around the assistant trainer.

Ryne Sandberg and Brian Dayett on an off day at Jody Davis's home in Atlanta. Look at Ryno's legs. He was a much faster runner than most think.

Ryne Sandberg's son, making sure Taytum and I know where Harry Caray sings "Take Me Out to the Ball Game."

Getting the players together for a team picture is difficult, but trying to get their kids together for a team picture is much more challenging. Taytum is sitting at the end of the group.

My former wife Sandy, our daughter Taytum, and me.
A very happy day at Wrigley Field. I want her to be a pitcher.
Sandy wants her to be a hitter. Taytum doesn't care.

Johnny Oates, now the manager of the Texas Rangers, by the mound,
was playing catch with Ron Cey until Taytum went after the ball.

LaMarr Hoyt and I having a Heineken at my rental home in Tatum Canyon in Phoenix. My neighbors at the mountain home were Joe Garagiola, Sr., and the late Erma Bombeck.

Gary Matthews, my locker partner for three years and close friend. Gary is now announcing for the Toronto Blue Jays, and his son, Gary, Jr., is now in the Cubs minor league system.

That's my dad in the shorts and swim trunks. He's clowning with a friend
whose name I don't know. Dad was always having fun.

	1	2	3	4	5	6	7	8	9	R	H	E
Visitor	0	0	0	1	0	1	0					
Home	1	0	2	1	0	0	0					

Squeeze Play

My finger healed faster than my damaged confidence. The line drive that almost hit me in the head may have been what I needed. There was relief in sight.

When my hand returned to normal, the Mariners sent me to Calgary, the Triple-A affiliate, to rehab for three weeks. I told Billy Connors, the pitching coach, "I think I might give some of my money back to the Mariners."

Billy said, "Don't be ridiculous, Steve. You're not going to give any money back."

As soon I arrived there, the Canadian papers did a story on "Steve Trout, the highest-paid athlete in Canada." It was true. I was making more than Wayne Gretzky or anyone else up there. But the trip to Calgary was a blessing, a catharsis for me. It took me away from the pressure, and I worked myself back into pitching shape — mentally. I felt confident again. The media and even Billy were gone, and I was going to do it by myself.

The Calgary team was that: a team. Guys hung with each other after the game and talked, a major difference from the bigs.

When I arrived, I met Arlene, one of the front-office staff people for the team, and I was convinced I had just met the most beautiful woman I'd ever seen. We started dating soon afterward. She gave me such a good feeling that I lost all my inner doubts, fears and loneliness. My

After five weeks, I was pitching better and went back to the Mariners. My first game was in Detroit, where we all know my worst inning was and Rick Cerone's, too. All of a sudden, I settled in on that Tiger Stadium mound, and I ended up pitching a good game and winning. I just prayed and prayed and prayed, and I pitched six and a third innings and got a win. Arlene and I were great until I started traveling with the Mariners. Then distance got in the way. I think she felt I used her. I called her after the season and had hopes of seeing her; however, she said never to call her again. It just didn't work out. We had different plans. I wanted to find happiness with baseball again. She wanted to be an intern in the White House. I hope she succeeded, then got out of there before Clinton moved in.

The Mariners and I weren't long for each other either.

* * *

After 19 games in '89, the Mariners and I parted ways. They traded Mark Langston to Montreal, bringing in a few pitchers in his place — Randy Johnson, Brian Holman, and Gene Harris — and I got bumped. I had gone 4-3 with a 6.60 ERA and three starts. The Mariners called me in and asked if I wanted to go to Triple-A or become a free agent. At that time in my career, I could veto a demotion, so I went for free agency, thinking somebody would give me a shot. But nobody called. I remained in Seattle for four weeks, hoping for the phone to ring and grabbing the best of what Seattle had to offer as a beautiful city.

In *The Baseball Encyclopedia* , my name's listed on the same page as my dad and Virgil "Fire" Trucks, who was on the Tigers staffs of the 1940s with my dad and was one of his good friends.

Paul "Dizzy" Trout. Father of Steve Trout. 15 years. 170-161 career record. 3.23 career ERA. Pitched in 521 games, started 322. Five times, he pitched more than 220 innings in a season, a feat that would be Herculean in today's game. In 1944, my dad threw a league-high 35½" innings, or about 39 games from start to finish. In fact, he finished 33 games that year, one more than I did for my whole 12-year career.

Steve "Rainbow" Trout. Son of Dizzy Trout. 12 years. 88-92 career record. 4.18 career ERA. Pitched in 301 games, started 236. 1,502 innings pitched. Pitched 200-plus innings in a season once, 1980.

Comparing our stats says as much about the differences in the game as it does the differences in the men. When I started my career, I told people in the media that if I would have half the career my dad did, then I'd still be successful. "Be careful what you ask for, you just might get it." I wonder if I programmed myself to have only half the career he had. Back then, baseball was survival of the fittest. When a pitcher took the mound to start a game, he was expected to finish it or be taken out of the game scratching and clawing. That was the way of the world. If you wanted something done right, you did it yourself.

Dad was a product of his time, a survivor. He cared for his arm himself, with no sports medicine staff or Tommy John surgery to bail him out. He bought his own spikes. He negotiated his own contracts. He did it all because nobody else would do it for him.

For me, things were different. Baseball wasn't a matter of survival like it was for Dad. When you travel to the Dominican Republic, parts of Puerto Rico, and Venezuela, you see those kids playing baseball, some of them, like Sammy Sosa, with a milk carton for a glove, dreaming of the ball and bat giving them a better life, like my dad did. A hungry man is a dangerous man. I had already had a comfortable childhood and signed for a bonus when I was drafted. I didn't see baseball as my way out, like my father did and the Latin kids do.

I didn't earn a degree to play baseball, or work my way up through the maze of minor leagues. I didn't throw honeydew melons in the back of a truck. My arm was a gift from God, and when baseball reached its warm hand out to me, I grabbed it and held on for the ride. At that time, I was 18 and making several times more money than kids my age who did go to college.

Once Jerry Seinfeld said that when men change TV channels with the remote control, they don't care about what's on; they only care about what *else* is on. That was me in my baseball life, my private life, and my business life. Most of the time my attention was not on what I was doing, but what else I could be doing or what I was going to do next. I guess I need to always feel challenged. There was a comment made about Walter Payton after his death, that he was into a lot of businesses and different ventures, always on the go. That's a lot like me, but that may be the only similarity between "Sweetness" and me.

Figuring out what to do next was my first order of business. I knew one thing well: baseball. And as I thought about Dad, and the way baseball was being played, and the way it ought to be played, I have some thoughts about how it all could be better.

First off, one percent should be taken out of the contract of any player making more than $2 million. Baseball should then take that money and donate it to kids. One place to put the money would be into youth baseball programs. You can already see that the NHL is trying to win over a generation by sponsoring a nationwide street hockey program. Baseball has Little League, but not every community can afford quality fields or uniforms or equipment. Baseball should buy tickets for kids whose families can't afford them, and let them see the games for free. Baseball could make that money go a long way, and it would see a payoff later. In 1996, the players developed the Major League Baseball Trust for Children. The trust, arranged by the players, recognizes a player, like Greg Maddux, who for the last three years has won the Players' Choice Award for outstanding pitcher in the National League. Greg has selected the Carnie Steele Pitts Home, Inc., in Atlanta for his grant. Players can designate a gift through the trust and enjoy tax protection. In 1998, the players started a program called "Gotcha Covered," a program partnership with licensees to provide baseball caps to children facing cancer-related challenges. Also, in 1999, "Cover All Bases" began to provide merchandise provided by licensees and player visits to hospitalized children in Major League cities. Programs like these are very encouraging. The kids are the game's future, and baseball is doing things to recognize that — finally. You can check it out by going to *www.bigleaguers.com* on the internet.

Baseball should get back to basics. Everybody has their little gimmick these days. Either it's the wrap-around sunglasses; or the long gold chain with the player's number on it; or the Nike shoes more suited for fashion than for running the bases; or the earring with the diamond stud. It's to the point where baseball is turning into an advertising contest. Who can wear the most peripheral stuff and make the most money doing it? I'm afraid baseball might turn into what auto racing has become — a "sport" of sponsorship and endorsements. They're even talking about the day when a player will be selling his right shoulder to one sponsor, his left to another, and making $50,000 on each one. It shouldn't be like that. Baseball is a simple game played by men who wear uniforms for a reason; they are a team, a well-oiled machine working toward a common goal.

Baseball players should sell the game more, and they should stop being so greedy about signing autographs. So what if a kid brings in 10 bucks for selling a ball with your name on it? It's worth it. And if it is too much for a player to handle, all they need to do is shake hands with the fans. That's all. It's free, it can't be sold, and it's an honest way of saying, "Hey, I'm here at the game, and it's really nice to meet you," or, "Hey, I'm glad you came to the ballpark to see me play today. It's nice to have a chance to say a few words with you before the game starts." All it would cost the players is a little time and courtesy.

Players should realize that it's not cheap for a family to attend a Major League game today. Most average people are now turning their sights to minor league and independent baseball because they can afford to go to more games and they can build a friendship with the younger players. A family of four spends an average of $120 to attend a Major League baseball game. For a night at a minor league park, that same family can get better seats and only spend $20-$30. They can attend four or five minor league games for the price of one Major League game. Am I idealistic? Yes. I don't know much about market share or any of those other complicated advertising terms, but I do know what baseball needs, and that's a return to a place where players see the fans as part of their paycheck; a place where they would graciously accept a chocolate cake baked just for them; a place where the owner of the team would have his phone number listed in the phone book, the way Bill Veeck did.

But my idealism and ideas about baseball weren't going to pay any bills. So on my way home from the Northwest in June of 1989, I sat down with a friend of mine who owns a real estate business and develops properties around the world. He was a good friend and a bright businessman. He had helped me uncover some complicated financial partnerships I was involved in. He knew a lot more about these investments than I did, and warned me about the future of them. He helped me avoid the potential damage they could do if I kept them. He brought me out on his boat, which was called, "Stratus," and we talked about the future. I mentioned the possibility of following his lead, becoming a real estate developer and finding properties around the world to develop. "You don't know much about that," he said. "You know baseball. You know people. What about becoming an agent?" I respected his opinion and took his suggestion. I decided that's what I'd do.

Over the next few months, I assembled a team consisting of an accountant, a lawyer, an accountant, a stockbroker, and an advisor to the business operation, and in November of 1989, I incorporated as United Sports Management.

Part of my decision to be an agent was because I felt I had some contributions to make, that I would uncover a lot of disgruntled athletes on the baseball diamond. I wanted to discover them to save them from the financial problems that I was having. The other part of the decision was that I thought it just made sense. The players who would sign with me would be in good hands. The ones who had bad representation and did not know how to get out of it; I wanted to help them find a way out.

Soon after incorporating, I got on an airplane and flew to Miami, with a case of the flu and a fever of 101 degrees, to see the

Caribbean World Series. I had my brochures and information about our company, anything to lure the stars of tomorrow.

On my first trip, I found out just how much I had to learn about my new profession. I went to the ball park, still suffering from a nasty case of the flu, and found a seat. A few spots ahead of me sat Gene Michael, manager of the Cubs during my last two seasons in Chicago. I said, "Hey, Stick, it's Steve Trout? How are you doing?"

"Hey," he said. "I haven't seen you since you got traded in '87. What are you doing down here?"

"I'm an agent," I said. "I just started a company, and I'm down here looking for players. What are you doing these days?"

"I'm the assistant general manager for the Yankees," he said. "If you're an agent, you should know that already." He was right.

I felt terrible and unprepared, but I knew I had to work hard. I was determined to let people know what my new venture was, being a sports agent. It was an *adventure*. I knew I had a lot to learn. I would have liked to have had a little more mentorship from a business person about what I could do with my life after the game, but so far, it has been trial and error.

The cruel and ruthless nature of the business was something I wasn't prepared for. One of my partners and I broke off our relationship because he had horrible communication skills. I had trained him two years in the business, and I brought in some major league clients. After our amicable breakup, many of our players decided to stay with him. However, I believe he manipulated me by not having my name on the player contracts, as we had agreed to in our oral contract. My only problem was I had no written agreement, so we could be going to a judge who I hope will find me being an equal partner of the players I brought into the company.

In this business, there's wheeling and dealing, people going behind each other's backs, other agents trying to get your clients, doing whatever they can to steal the fruits of your labor.

One player I represented was Marshall Bose, who was with the Brewers at the time. I went to Indianapolis when he was in Triple-A to see him. He said he was going to leave my company because when other agents called him and he said I was his agent, they laughed. They would attack me any way they could.

Most agents are smooth talking con artists. "He doesn't know a thing about the business," they say. "Why don't you get someone who knows what they're doing?" They plant a bad seed, and unfortunately, some of the players can't see past that. Players should look very deeply into their agents' backgrounds, being very careful of the financial side of things. I have a file of great con jobs done on athletes from all sports with what their financial planner-agents have done to them.

Former Detroit Tigers pitcher Walt Terrell filed suit against a Skokie financial advisor who represented a host of pro athletes. His suit was a racketeering case that accused Talent Services, Inc., of fraudulent, negligent, and inept management.

Tampa Bay Buccaneers wide receiver Gordon Jones won a judgement of $300,000 from TSI.

Former New York Met Keith Hernandez filed suit against TSI also.

Hall of Famer Mike Webster of the Pittsburgh Steelers was homeless for a year or two because his money was blown by a financial advisor.

Larry Roberts, who played for the San Francisco 49ers, put his trust in Brian Smith, a former player with the Minnesota Vikings and Los Angeles Rams, and lost a lot of money in bad investments. Later, Roberts was awarded more than $220,000.

I expected a little more commitment from my clients, more appreciation of what I do. I don't necessarily blame the players for changing agents. I blame the other people in the business who continue to badmouth just for their own gain. It's just like the mudslinging in a political campaign. It gets very nasty.

For example, I did a young player's Wilson glove contract: Danny Kolb, from Sterling, Illinois, who throws 97 miles an hour and went on to play for the Texas Rangers. I called Danny during the wintertime to check up on him because he was sleeping in his car. I was always taking care of him and staying on him to make sure he was working out. He was with me at least a year in A ball. A few years ago, when he went to Double-A, I got a call from Brad Arnsberg, a pitching coach who was my teammate with the Yankees, who said, "Steve, someone's trying to cut your grass. Boras has one of his guys down here." When Scott Boras comes after your client, it's hard to compete. Boras can have one of his hired guns all over your client, and he can plant a seed in that player that he's represented the big names in the game. When it comes down to it, he does what he wants.

Player agents are a silent group of guys who have a lot of henchmen on the side who do the dirty work. They go down to Florida and Arizona and steal and bribe players. They'll co-sign on cars, tell them, "Whatever you need, we'll pay for it." They cut checks. You give a Latin kid $5,000, and he's yours, and the agents know they're going to make that money back four or five times over, sometimes immediately. I've seen an agent taking seven players in a convertible to a mall, letting them shop on a budget in order to sign them. They were all rookies, all Latin players. The ones from the Dominican Republic and Venezuela are especially subject to this type of a sales pitch because they don't go in the draft, while Puerto Rican players do. Agents cover those fertile grounds of Venezuela and the Dominican like a hawk after healthy prey, searching for the young kid they can send to the highest bidder. Some agents are corporations and even have camps set up in these areas to showcase their latest talents to the highest-bidding team. A young American draft choice asked me after I told him I was an agent, "If I sign with you, does that mean I have to pay you the three percent my agent took of my bonus?" Some kids receive only a $40,000 bonus, and I would never take a penny of that. Other agents would, in a New York minute. I explained to him not to pay the agent and file a grievance. I simply don't believe in taking a percentage of any player's bonus that is less than $100,000.

I've seen how some Latin players have had four or five agents at the same time just so they could take advantage of the free equipment they'd receive. The only way to clarify it was to ask the general manager to call the player and have him to declare specifically who is agent is.

I've had some Major Leaguers, and lost them, too. I had Enrique Wilson, Danny Patterson, Scott Eyre, Jesse Garcia, Tony Saunders, and others. Normally, when you receive a letter from one of your clients, it's not a birthday card, but instead a termination of the contract.

The agent market is burgeoning like the ever expanding market of baseball is. Today, over 20% of big leaguers are of Latin descent, and more are coming from the Pacific Rim than ever. Agents will have to move in those directions also. I believe some day baseball will have a global league that will be under the Major League Baseball aegis. World Cup-type tournaments will be very likely. The envoy and pitch-hit-and-run programs are already established to help expand the growing inter-national market. Huge increases in worldwide product sponsorship have driven merchandise sales up over 35%. Major League Baseball now has an office in London to help with the growing European market.

Japan is still the strongest country in Major League Baseball licensed sales. Knowing all this, I guess I'd better update my passport.

Major League Baseball has become very international in the last two decades with players from 16 different countries. Presently, only the flags of the United States and Canada are flown in the Major League parks. I believe Major Baseball should adopt a policy where all the flags of the players' countries are flown in the parks. I've already petitioned Major League Baseball to have this done.

If an agent has a problem with another agent stealing his players, then you might be able to go to court on the tortious interference of a contract; however, the Players' Association has an internal system that patches over the dispute. This internal system is an arbitrary way of keeping the matter from the public.

When I started my new career, I had a hard time with other agents. Almost 95% of them never even smelled a big league locker room. I still believe former players surrounded by the right experts in business make the ideal representatives for an athlete.

I'm not proud to call myself an agent. It's a glorified title, for sure. I'm proud of what I do as an advisor to the players. I'm an advisor who knows the business, and I get compensation from the players for making sure they get top dollar. My strength lies in my connection to the game: my knowledge of the game, my experience in arbitration, being a free agent — twice — and being traded — three times. I know the ups and downs a player goes through. Also, being a former player, my ties to the Players Association are strong, and they provide the information I need to represent my player in the best possible way. My relationships with GMs and owners are more personal than most agents out there. I'll get the same dollar Scott Boras would get. I truly believe that. I keep files on players who sign record-breaking contracts at their position and players who sign early for long-term deals. Getting the best deal for my client is my goal.

Nobody can do more for a client than me because I've been through everything they're going through.

Steve Boras got Alex Rodriguez the largest contract ever at over $250 million. I believe I could have convinced Mr. Hicks, the Texas Rangers owner, after reviewing his financial statement, that A-Rod is worth more than that. Mr. Hicks is a businessman who believes he can pay his players anything he wants and pass the cost on to the fans. This sort of thinking is the reason spending is out of control. I see the whole 30 teams having major problems. Eventually, I believe there will be fewer teams in baseball. Maybe 16 teams will survive. Baseball is in trouble when guys like Boras can convince owners to overpay players and do it without holding a gun to their heads. The successful baseball owners should be ashamed of themselves for giving that kind of money to one player.

* * *

Playing pro ball was just like living at home, except I had more domestic help. The challenge each day as a big leaguer is to jump out of bed to get where you're supposed to be. Like Woody Allen said, "Ninety percent of the job is showing up." People set out your uniform for you each day, wash your clothes, cook your food, drive you where you need to go. The bed is never unmade. If you're a pitcher, you have a catcher to call signs for you. The ultimate goal: a quality start, six innings giving up three runs or less. If the game starts to slip away, sitting in the outfield is a bullpen — people who are paid to trot into the game and help you out. Why should I go the distance? Why should I chart pitches or analyze batters on my off days? Someone else could do it. Now I realize if someone always comes to your aid, then you wait for it, even expect it. If you're not born with the ability to "close," whether it's on the mound or in life, it's a hard habit to learn. Life is made of little habits. Having discipline is very important. I surely wasn't disciplined as a ballplayer, but today I know that. There's a saying: "We grow old too soon, smart too late."

The result of this half-hearted approach is that your personal growth slows to a crawl. Interpersonal skills, if you possess any at all, become unnecessary. The coaches aren't really talking to you about life; they're teaching you how to get four more inches on your fastball. A team meeting is not a discussion on the planning for the future. It's normally a yelling match where the GM threatens to send you to the minors or — as Dallas Green did once — promises to send you back to the old locker room at Wrigley Field if you don't straighten up.

When people saw Steve Trout, the Major League ballplayer, they saw someone who was disorganized and undisciplined. I would pitch on the days I was supposed to pitch, and the other four days I wouldn't pay as much attention to the game as I should have. I got very bored watching the game. I would head into the locker room a lot, just hanging out in the players lounge during the game. I should have been a better student of the game. Baseball makes it easy to create loose ends in life. Everything is Broadway. You travel across the country, first class, with the best of everything. Alcohol was always on planes, and often so were drugs. The bathrooms on the planes were the only place you could go fire up, so sometimes you would have to bring cologne with you to spray after you left. Or you could hold down the drain on the small sink, and the opening in the drain would pull the smoke down and out of the room, leaving not so much as a scent.

Marriage — especially young marriage — and baseball are not a fair match. Players start to think they are bigger than life, and the attention they receive is matched only by rock stars. Pretty soon, the road trips get long and lonely, and when you stay at the finest hotels in New York or Montreal or Atlanta or San Diego, believe me, there are a lot of pretty women. Sometimes, you start questioning yourself, and you think, "Hey, this woman is prettier than my wife." Other times, you just want the sex.

Women were available in every city. Everyone cracked jokes a few years ago when Wilt Chamberlain claimed to have slept with 20,000 women, but if you look at a 30-year span with 365 days in a year, he'd have to sleep with two women each day. There were probably days he slept with six or seven in one day. That's not as crazy as everyone thinks. Only he knew how accurate his math was. But I can tell you that if Rafael Palmeiro or David Justice or Mark Grace or some of the other good-looking players wanted to start that kind of pace, they could do it, too. In my day, George Brett could have gotten laid 20 times a day. When he'd return to the hotel each day after a road game, a stack of messages two inches thick would be waiting for him. Other guys had no trouble picking up usherettes in St. Louis, Montreal, and other parks.

Some players — like Carlton Fisk — would bring girls on road trips. They'd pay for their plane tickets. The girls would show up for one thing: lots of sex. We called it "importing."

The women don't care that they're one of many. They say, "I don't care who you're screwing, screw me because you are who you are." Many ballplayers strayed from the course. If you did, your sense of morality would eat at you. Other guys didn't worry about it. Some guy saw it as an ego thing, a statistical thing. People are always battling their inner dummies. It amazes me why we do some of the things we do — some stupid things indeed. It's all related to our ego.

I never had a real promiscuous lifestyle, but yeah, there were times it happened. I'm not happy about what I did, but looking back, it could have been worse. I remember Jay Baller, a relief pitcher with the Cubs, saying to me, "Hey, Steve, I got a problem. I have to go out and get laid every night." I told him what Reggie Jackson told me. "You can drink and play ball, or you can hunt women all night. But if you do both, you will kill your career." It hurt Jay's.

Back then, I didn't realize how off-base I was. Walking down the aisle with Sandy at age 20 seemed like the right thing to do. She was my first true love, and I wanted to marry her. If I had it to do over again, I would do it the same way. We have a daughter who is the greatest gift God could give anybody. Sandy was a good wife. More than a dozen years later, I still realize that. She was committed to being a friend and a wife. She is a great mother. And she was faithful and spiritual. At the age of 27, though, those were not the things I wanted. The temptations were too plentiful, and they caused me to lose interest in what was important. Years later, I understood that without the three "F" words in your vocabulary — faith, family, and friends — life isn't nearly as rich or fulfilling.

That revelation didn't come to me overnight. After my playing career was over in 1990 and I was separated from Sandy and Taytum, my life challenges were seeing how many exciting places I could travel to and how many rounds of golf I could squeeze into a week. My putting stroke became a priority. I was determined to make my new agent business, United Sports Management, one of the best in the country. That was great for a while. But by 1994, while I was still determined to succeed as a sports advisor, the sense of accomplishment just wasn't there.

Sometimes, it takes a tragedy to make reality smack you upside the head.

That moment happened to me late in 1994. I was in Florida on Thanksgiving Day that year when I received a call that my mother was in the hospital. She was in for 11 days. The fourth day I went to visit her at 10 a.m. I remember it was 10 a.m. because it was crucial for me to hit my tee-off time at noon. Mom told me her condition in only a way she could. "I've got the same thing Jackie O(nassis) has," she said, putting a happy face on her despair. "I've got lymphoma." She was laid to rest on December 7, "Pearl Harbor Day," almost as if she had planned it that way. The singer at the 75th birthday party we'd had for her the year before sang at her funeral. Her party was very special. It was a surprise party with about 200 friends and family. We wanted to give her a special present. We gave her an honorary degree from the "University of Life Experience" with doctorate degrees in medicine for curing our colds and healing our cuts; in economics for keeping Converse All-Stars on our feet and always a tremendous dinner on the table on a shoe-string budget; in psychology for solving our problems with ease and helping us find answers to all life's challenges; in culinary arts for making Bob chipped beef, Ross a crisp bacon sandwich, and me pancakes in the shape of my initials; in education for helping us with our homework for more than 20 years.

People said kind words about her at the service, and when it was over, everyone in attendance gave her a standing ovation. The funeral director said he'd never seen that before, a standing ovation for the deceased. The day of the burial it was cold and rainy with no sun shining. But when the casket was being placed into the ground, just as it was being lowered, the sun came out, clear and bright as could be. I made a comment, "Mom, you'll get a suntan up there, too." Mom was a sun goddess, always featuring a most beautiful suntanned face. Everyone in attendance was stunned by that moment, when the sun came out of nowhere so she could bask in it on earth one last time. I knew it was her spirit entering heaven and she was all right.

Mom was gone; and Steve Trout, a man with six brothers and three sisters, was an orphan, alone in the world.

A mother has a way of keeping the little boy in you alive, and when she's gone, the boy in you dies, too. I had nowhere to turn and nobody to guide me.

My family, large as it is, has never been as supportive as you'd expect. With so many kids in the family, it seems like we each have our eggs spread evenly, and few of us have that snug relationship with a brother or sister that a smaller family would have. There's so much chatter, and my relationships with my brothers and sisters haven't changed very much since I stopped playing. I always tell my brother Paul, who was my closest family friend, how I always get phone calls when people need things.

There's no hate or animosity or anger. It's not bad blood; it's the lack of blood. It's more like indifference. In a way, it's better to be 2,000 miles away in Bozeman, Montana, and not see someone than to be 20 miles away and not see them. It gives you an excuse to be passive, to not care. At Thanksgiving dinner, people would get up after the meal and go their own way. There was no deep, deep conversation in the family, which is a shame, because we have a great connection to history, but we just don't cut it as a close family.

When Mom died, so did the family.

Maybe it's that some of my family resented my baseball ability and what I did — or didn't do — with it. One brother in particular, Bob, always felt I could do better. He knew I was running around with some wrong people, like he was, and I was ruining my career. He was working at Pullman Steel on Chicago's Southeast Side, and he absorbed a lot of social pressure from Cubs and Sox fans because of me. Some of it was good, some bad. But Bob never gave me the freedom to be who I was. I remember once walking into my brother Bob's room and seeing an article that quoted Carton Fisk saying that "A lot of these players have Steve Trout Syndrome." I was hurt by that. It was a negative article, and Bob had it up in his room as if to say, "See, I knew I was right."

John was more envious than jealous, and being a year older and looking like me he was wondering, "Why couldn't it have been me?" John was a dancer, lived in the nightclubs for a while, and beat the crap out of a bouncer who was bad-mouthing me. He lives in the past, and he has an eccentric personality. If you go to his house, a few miles from mine, you have to leave a note and make an appointment to see him. He saves everything: tapes, boxes, things you accumulate when you buy something. When we helped him move it was one of the saddest days of my life. He was living like a pack-rat. He's an extremely intelligent individual with a good heart. Something just happened, maybe his identity was challenged by me. I was a movie star and he wasn't. People said, "Your brother did this," and, "Your brother did that," to the point where he has a deep-seeded anger that surfaces from time to time. My brothers and sisters wonder how we can help him. I think we should take more responsibility for what happens to any family member, but most don't care. Maybe their own struggles are enough for them to worry about. I care about John, and I remember that his opinion was highly respected by everyone. Today, he's very paranoid with frequent personality changes.

Through the years, Rich was probably my most supportive brother. Paul lives in Bozeman, Montana, and wouldn't get the news until the Pony Express brought it there. He was never one to call me up about the games. He would write a letter instead. My brother Rich and I discuss John the most.

I played in Chicago for eight years, and the reason we were a closer family then was because mom was the cement and the mix. Now, there's no feeling of that. Since Mom died, we haven't had Thanksgiving as a family. Not once. Everybody goes their own way. Occasionally, Ross and Pat play tennis, but Ross and I never play unless Pat is in town. I'm close to my sister Connie. John's lost in a world of fictional reality and prefers to live like a hermit. Bob bought the house after mom died and sold it a couple of years ago. The last link to our family legacy is gone.

As for myself, I live in a nice, single-family house in Munster, Indiana. It's no ballplayer's mansion. It's an attractive middle-class house on a suburban street with other people who are dentists and teachers and salespeople. I like my home, and I feel comfortable there. But it's not a house built for entertainment. I always say it's going to take another death to bring us all together again, but it's to the point where my family are becoming strangers to me, and I question if anything can bring us together again.

Thinking about my mom and my family and my career has its depressing moments. The darkest days started in October of 1995 and went through January of 1996, when every day I waged a war against my feelings, trying to unearth the sense of loss and grief. It felt like a ball of sorrow welling up in my stomach and reminding me that I don't have anyone in the whole world. My daughter's birthday triggered everything. As Taytum turned 13, I realized that she was at the age I was when my dad died. All I could think about was me dying before she would turn 14, and leaving her fatherless, which triggered the grief I held inside from the loss of my mother and father. I was going through a double grieving, which made the experience so powerful.

For those few months from October to January, I unleashed all the feelings of grief that I had hid from for almost 25 years after losing my dad. As Taytum became 13, I saw changes in her that blew my mind. She was growing into a beautiful woman, and she helped me stay strong, as she always has.

Most people who saw me then wouldn't have realized my sullen condition. I never stayed in bed or dreaded the start of the day, like some people. Ordinary people running into me wouldn't have noticed a change. But I sure did. That period was a cleansing, a healing, a catharsis I had never experienced before. Boom! It was like running into a brick wall, over and over. Boom! I'd scout a baseball game, things would pop into my brain, and I would have a hard time remembering where I was or why I was there.

For three months, I couldn't sleep. If I was sleeping, I was not even aware of it. All I was doing was praying. Thinking. Trying to figure it out. I was finally learning that it was okay to grieve. I was actually grieving everything I had held inside me for all those years. I think it's common for people to hold in their feelings, and by doing that, they create excuses for bad habits — overdrinking, being hostile, not being compassionate. Finding the grief was my way of letting go. When I accepted that it was grief, then I could stop holding it in and fighting it, and I became a better person.

When this friend of mine turned 12 years old, his father brought him onto his fishing boat on Lake Michigan and put him to work pulling up nets. My friend did that for the next 25 years. I saw him recently, and he's still holding in anger that he was taken away from his childhood. He never got to participate in all the things that boys get to do, and he has anger toward his younger brother, who didn't have to work as hard as he did, maybe because his father realized what a mistake he had made. My friend can't let go of all this, and today, even though he's financially secure, he's suffering inside and has destructive ten-dencies toward himself and other people. If he doesn't learn how to let go, I'm afraid those destructive tendencies will get the best of him. The same way he used to search for fish, he should now search for a way to let go.

Seeing all this has taught me a lot about how far I have come and how I now can help those people like my friend.

For me, the healing began when Mom died. When it was over, my spirit had cleansed itself. I called every member of my family and apologized for things I had done years ago. I told Ross I was sorry for the way I treated him, handing down the terrors of big-brother domination. I wrote to Sandy to apologize for who I was and what I had done to her when we were married. I called my sister Laura. I drove to Tennessee and talked to my sister Diane, who helped me see the beauty of what we all had.

Just as importantly, I began to come to terms with myself and my underwhelming baseball career. In the final analysis, God may have given me one of the greatest left arms in history, but he sure made the rest of my career one hell of a climb.

After Dad died, my grandmother and my mother raised me, and when I entered pro ball, I was an easy target. The dominant male figure was missing, and without Dad there to guide me, I followed the times without considering the consequences. Looking back, I wasn't ready for the Major Leagues, the same way I wasn't ready for marriage, either. In my first years with the White Sox when I stood on the mound between innings and looked into the right field stands at old Comiskey Park to see rowdy, beer-breathed guys brawling, I was affected by it. The security guys in their bright yellow coats would be ready to throw them into the holding room, and I would stand on the mound and gaze out there and think, "Why do they have to do that? Why do they have to fight?" I wasn't focused on slipping a slider past Reggie Jackson. I was contemplating the frailties of human nature in the bottom of the sixth inning.

That stuff wouldn't have affected Dad one bit. But that was just it. He wasn't there to beat my ass when I strayed from the course. I don't blame myself entirely. Much of it was my environment. I chose the wrong role models, the wrong friends. I didn't realize at the time what a great career I was hurting. With Dad around, there would have been someone to help me control the pressures of the lifestyle. When Ron Schueler messed with me, Dad would have provided me the advice on not just how to weather that storm, but how to prevail through it.

Instead, Dad was gone. Mom is gone. And I'm still here, Looking at myself and seeing the growth I've made. After baseball, it's hard for the feelings of those special moments of the game to be duplicated.

Baseball and its Major League money don't answer life's questions. It just makes those questions more difficult to ask. At age 40, I was asking myself questions that most people ask at 18. It's hard to understand, I know. I imagine it's like a housewife who kisses her husband before he goes off to work every day for 20 years, sends the kids off to college, then stops, takes a deep breath, and looks around and wonders sadly where all the years went and wrestles with that quintessential question that I ask myself. "What will I do now with the rest of my life?"

	1	2	3	4	5	6	7	**8**	9	R	H	E
Visitor	0	0	0	1	0	1	0	0				
Home	1	0	2	1	0	0	0	0				

Set-Up Man

Where you head in life so often depends on the decisions you make: how you act, who you hang out with, how you spend your time. The forks in the road come often, and one wrong turn can leave you miles from your destination.

One of my toughest challenges has been when I wasn't battling my own inadequacies inside my own head, other people did it for me. That's the way it is when people label you a "flake" or a "space case." No matter what you do, when you've earned that tag, it's yours for keeps.

When I was with the Sox, a friend came looking for me and asked Bobby Winkles, our third base coach, where I was. Winkles pointed up at the night sky and said, "He's up there on the moon." Actually, I was right behind him in the dugout. This was the attitude a lot of coaches and people seemed to have toward me, which made playing for them all the harder for me.

Bill Buckner won't be remembered as a perennial .300 hitter, but as the guy who let the 1986 World Series roll through his legs. Leon Durham will always be remembered for that one error in the 1984 NLCS, instead of the many good years he had. I'll always be remembered as the free-spirited left-handed pitcher who had everyone wondering whether he'd throw a one-hitter or not make it through three innings. Mostly it would be something that people would expect from the notorious actions of a lefty. Actually, some of my idiosyncracies came as a shield, to protect myself from letting people know who I really am.

Ryne Sandberg had a very thick, protective shell, too, but I portrayed some of the image that came with my father's nickname, "Dizzy." I truly believe it was part of a curse, in a way, for me. Baseball people and media alike had already labeled me. If I did something wrong, it would be, "Well, what do you expect? It's Dizzy's kid?" If I did something right, it would be, "Yeah, but he'll never be as good as his father was."

One story in particular dogs me to this day, and even though it's been newspaper fodder for years now, it isn't true: The time Steve Trout injured himself falling off a stationary bike. That's right, a stationary bike. The whole thing has been blown out of proportion by miles, so let me set the record straight.

In 1985, the year Pete Rose was breaking Ty Cobb's all-time hit record, the Reds were in town for a series at Wrigley. The press box was jammed, and rightfully so. Rose was only six hits away from tying the record, and history could be made that weekend. In the first two games against us, Rose managed four hits, so he was two hits away from tying the record heading into the Sunday game I was supposed to pitch. At this stage later in his career, Rose wasn't playing against lefties, so he planned to sit for the Sunday game and return to Cincinnati for a series starting on Monday, perfect for a couple of standing-room-only crowds back at Riverfront Stadium. Knowing that Rose wouldn't play Sunday, the media raced for the airport and started booking hotel rooms in Cincinnati.

After Saturday's game, I drove back to my house in Crete. I had an urge to squeeze in a quick bike ride with Sandy and Taytum before the sun went down. So, soon after I was in the door I yelled, "Sandy, let's go for a bike ride!" My wife grabbed her bike and put Taytum on hers. I jumped on mine, and we were off for a bike ride near our house on a barely paved road with gravel on the shoulders.

All excited to be out pedaling with my family, I couldn't help but try to make Taytum smile, and so I went into my act like Paul Newman in "Butch Cassidy and the Sundance Kid." I screwed around on the bike, turning around and looking at Taytum, trying to make her laugh. As I was doing my stunt routine, looking at her, I hit some gravel, and my bike went skidding across the rocks. I fell right on my left side and scraped it up pretty good. My very next thought was, "Oh, my God, I've got to pitch tomorrow. I've got to get some ice on this." I was torn up bad.

The next morning I went to the park knowing damn well I couldn't pitch, but I was too scared to say anything. Hundreds of reporters were rushing to Cincinnati to be ahead of the story, and I didn't want the media to know why all of a sudden the lefty who was supposed to keep Rose on the bench wasn't pitching. I wanted to keep it a secret, but I knew I couldn't get away with it. So an hour before the game I looked myself over, went up to Billy

Connors, and said, "Billy, something happened to me last night. I can't pitch."

I was scratched, figuratively and literally. The news hit the street like war had broken out. "Trout's not pitching! Trout's not pitching! Rose is going to play today after all!" All the media that had raced 100 miles an hour to the airport, now were racing 100 miles an hour back to the ballpark, and they had a terrible time trying to accommodate them because they had no credentials and it was game time. The parking was another nightmare. In short, there was total chaos.

That day, under an overcast, turbulent sky, Pete Rose tied Ty Cobb's record at Wrigley Field, all because of me. He almost broke the record in the ninth inning that day. After the game, word spread about how Trout fell off a bike. Everyone wanted interviews with me, but I turned them all down. Whitey Herzog, who was managing the Cardinals back then, said, "If Trout pitches great against us in St. Louis, we're going to send him a bike!" Marge Schott, the Reds owner, was the most furious because she was banking on Pete filling the house for both the tying and record-breaking hits.

Naturally, people ask me about Pete and the Hall of Fame. I used to feel differently, but now I believe he's paid his dues and deserves to be in the Hall.

For years, I couldn't go anywhere without some clown saying, "Hey! How's the bike?" It never stops, and even to this day, it's perpetuated by the fans and the media, and like Pinocchio's nose, it grows more and more as time goes on.

A few years ago, I picked up *The Chicago Tribune* and one of the columnists, Bob Verdi, had a story where he mentioned about the time Steve Trout fell off a "stationary bike," which as you now see is nowhere close to the truth.

Recently, Jon Lieber of the Cubs had an injury falling off a bike, and the story was dredged up again.

Looking back on the bike incident, I admit it's not one of my favorite memories. Even though it was blown out of proportion, that's the life athletes live in. Yes, I'd have done a few things differently, but who wouldn't? Time does that. It makes you see the road from a broader perspective, where you've been and where you're planning to go. As I entered my 40s, I didn't have the answers; but at least I was asking the questions. And I noticed something. The more I talked to people, the more I realized a lot of us are facing the same pain, although we often don't want to reveal ourselves much.

If there was anything that soothed my feelings during some of my troubled times, it was that I wasn't alone. Gary Matthews told me that Bobby Dernier was struggling within himself and trying to find his niche in life since his baseball career came to an end. But if any of Bobby's former teammates were to talk to him at a Cubs Convention or another function, they'd never know it. Guys just don't talk about stuff like that. It's like when you ask someone, "How are you doing?" People just reply, "Fine, how are you?" Or they say, "Okay." There are not many times you actually learn *how* they're doing. We should be more honest with our feelings, let people know the truth. I believe strongly in a saying I learned from Gus Hoefling, Steve Carlton's personal trainer: "Always stay within the boundaries of the truth and you shall do no wrong." I believe this is very true.

There's another saying that I believe in strongly. "Each one teach one." This means learning life's lessons from one another.

Seeing the way I and other ex-athletes struggle has taught me something: life is a lot about survival. That fact has made me understand my dad much more than I did before. Now it's almost as if I look back and want to be just like him: a provider, someone who had real maturity about him. Dad realized early on that life was a competition and you had to be tough out there. I feel that way, too.

Some people might question my toughness, but believe me, I always wanted to be the one on the mound when we needed a big win. I always wanted to do more to help the team. Sometimes my emotional side was so intense I'd treat my wins like losses and my losses like death.

When life gave me lemons, I picked them up and threw them right back. When I was drafted and went out on my own, I lacked the self-discipline to stay on the right track. When Tony LaRussa didn't understand why I was concerned about my sick grandmother, when Ron Schueler messed with my pitching repertoire, my way of retaliating — to rebel against authority — didn't hurt anyone but me. Sometimes I forced myself to swim upstream because inside me, I needed that struggle. I believe we create our own turmoil, just for the fight, and people who need stimulation do it more often.

I didn't realize at the time what a great career I was hurting. I don't blame myself. It was the times I grew up in and my environment. I chose the wrong role models, the wrong friends. Most of the people I hung out with from that time are spending the second half of their lives trying to recover from the first half. If given the chance, I'd change some of the things I did. But I can't. I can only fix the here and now, and so that's what I've devoted myself to every day: being prepared and organized, so I can grow as a person. This life isn't a rehearsal. When you have something special, don't let it go.

One year I was a participant as a coach in Randy Hundley's fantasy baseball camp in Mesa, Arizona, where I had a lot of fun because Joe Pepitone was there and he's a major cut-up and I really enjoyed seeing the campers living out there childhood dreams. Hundley, the catcher for the Cubs in the late 1960s and early '70s, said it best: "Make them tear the uniform off your back because, if you have any doubts that you hung it up too quickly, that can live with you forever." It's the same way in life. Make sure you live every day as if it were your last. If you leave something unfinished or have doubts, you will never feel complete and fulfilled.

I've learned that the most important questions are the ones you ask yourself. Dallas Green always said, "Look in the mirror." So do that. Look in the mirror. Do you like what you see? Are you challenging your heart and your mind to grow spiritually? Are you growing closer to your loved ones? Are you sharing some love and support with those less fortunate?

I've begun to create a better atmosphere for myself, to think about maybe remarrying and having a family. I have realized I have yet to be tapped or challenged as a person, and that I want to become someone who leaves some kind of a mark on this planet. I think of people who have overcome inconceivable obstacles — like the stories you'll see about the little boys who lost their hands to bombshells in Bosnia and how they've learned to hold a pen with their toes to write. Those kinds of inspirational stories only remind me of the itching I have inside to be a part of something, to contribute. As an advisor, I can help young players make better decisions. Maybe I can be the one that a young player can look back upon and say, "Yes, Steve Trout helped me as a player, but more as a man."

As for my own growth, I've started to pick my friends carefully. They didn't pick me. Maybe that's why I don't have too many. Friends mean a lot to me, yet it's hard to find someone you can really trust, depend on, who wants to be your friend for who you are and not for what you can do for them. To me, athletes face one of the most difficult battles, and that's finding people who are truly their friends and have a heart for them as a human being, not as a celebrity.

Drugs have left my life. Mom's death got me away from all that. I know that I still like a beer as much as the next guy, but I'm much more in control now.

At this time, I am a player recruiter for a successful agent business. I decided I wanted to help athletes improve their lives during their careers and after their careers are over. It makes me happy to help them avoid the mistakes I made. I began giving some of my time to kids, teaching them about baseball and whatever else they can learn from me. I have strived to be more hard-working, respected, self-reliant. I have taken college classes to learn more about the world and my place in it.

I have continued to focus on my number one priority: being a loving father to Taytum. My investment in our relationship continues to pay off. Any day I can walk into Sandy's house, go into Taytum's room, and talk to her about her feelings or what-ever is on her mind. Sandy told her husband that was the way it was going to be. Sometimes I'd make my dates sit in the back seat so Taytum could sit up front. When Taytum's in my car, she sits in the front seat — nobody else. Now that I think of it, that's a policy that's probably cost me a few relationships, but it's been well worth it. I continue to look for love, knowledge, and my own joys in life.

Slowly, I've planted seeds of reconciliation with the people and ideas most important to me, and relationships have begun to flower. That is, with the exception of one: baseball. The game was the family heirloom, passed down from Dad to me for love, respect, and safekeeping. But somewhere along the line, the heirloom changed, and my relationship with the game changed, too. In Dad's day, baseball was a romantic game played by men who cared about being ballplayers and being loyal to each other. In my day, baseball had evolved into an agent-dominated game, featuring men who didn't see themselves as ballplayers as much as entertainers and businessmen. As I began pulling my life together, I realized how much I wanted a reconciliation with baseball. I missed it.

I like baseball and the time of year it's played. I like the team approach, the inner workings of the infield and the most special part of the game, the double play. I like the relationships, the hidden communication behind the basic pickoff play. I like the feel of a baseball, the perfect roundness, the cowhide, the seams. I like the mathematical symmetry of the game: nine players, nine innings and three strikes, three outs. I like the way baseball from my dad's era, the '30s, '40s, and '50s. It was a very noble game, America's game, and I liked the way the fans of that era turned out and the way they dressed in suits and ties and Sunday hats. I like how each ballpark has a different look and a different charm. Each park has its own bundle of sounds and smells. I like the history of them all, the cut of the natural grass, the ivy, and the sprinklers that come on after the game. It's too bad the kids of today haven't had the chance to see the old ballparks like Comiskey Park or Tiger Stadium, but maybe they can see Wrigley Field, Yankee Stadium or Fenway Park before they decide to tear those down. Also, I like that you can be a fan of the National League or American and that there's a difference.

In the winter of 1996, on the recommendation of Bill Bryk, the Pirates sent me an invitation to try out for Spring Training 1997. After much thought, I accepted.

	1	2	3	4	5	6	7	8	9	R	H	E
Visitor	0	0	0	1	0	1	0	0	0	2	5	0
Home	1	0	2	1	0	0	0	0	X	4	8	1

Save Opportunity

Bradenton, Florida, February 28, 1997.

As I stood on the mound at the Pirates training complex, staring at my first Mexico City batter, I was a different pitcher than I was 20 years ago. At this stage of my life, I knew a little about the game, and I knew I needed a plan of attack and an approach to pitching. I knew I wasn't going to be a starter. If I were to make my improbable trip north with the big league team, it would be as a slider-throwing reliever. My thinking made sense.

During my Major League career, when my slider was on, it was one of the nastiest around, so my plan was a simple one to start: fastball, slider, maybe change speeds a little bit. That might have been my trouble in New York, I realized. I tried to do too much. I should have canned my fastball as an out pitch and just thrown the slider 85 percent of the time. Instead, anytime a left-handed hitter came up, I tried to throw the fastball by him. Maybe my pride got in the way, or there was a part of me that said, "Look, the fastball is what I came to the dance with, that is what I'll leave the dance with."

But now, at age 39, I knew better. If you're going to be a starter, 30 percent sliders. As a reliever, 50-50, or more. Sparky Lyle, the former Yankees star of the 1970s, used his slider 90 percent of the time toward the end of his career. Nobody had to tell me the slider was my best pitch, especially moving across the plate the way it did at 85 miles an hour.

As I went into the windup, I held the ball across the seams on the thin part of the ball, and it felt good. So did my mechanics. Bill Bryk made sure of that. In the weeks we had used to prepare for this day, we had refined and simplified my pitching motion to a basic 1-2-3, and with my arms in close I wasn't fighting myself as much as I had in my earlier career. It was easier to get my arm on top of the ball, and easier on my body. I was in control, balanced,

148

and heading toward home plate with everything working together.

The first guy up, a righty, swung at my first pitch, chopping it up the first-base line. How about that? The first batter I faced swung hard, and the ball went eight feet. He couldn't have rolled it any better. I reacted catlike, coming off the mound, snatching up the ball, spinning, and throwing just to the left of the runner for a perfect strike at first base. It was like I was saying, "Here I am, I'm ready," and it was a great feeling. It meant something. It wasn't like a little fly ball or ground out. It tested my old hamstrings, and I had great balance. All my pieces were still intact.

As I was pitching, I could hear Bill in the background yelling, "Look at that, Cam (Bonifay)! Ninety! Look at that, Cam! Ninety-one! He's the Lazarus Man! He's back! He's the Lazarus Man!"

The more I threw, the prouder Bill acted, and I understood why. He didn't do this because he's my friend, or because I needed a break. He put his credentials on the line to invite me, and now I was hitting 92 m.p.h. on the gun, with an 86 slider.

The first inning went easily. I threw only five pitches.

The second inning took more work. The cleanup hitter — a guy named Ty Gainey — clobbered a hanging slider over the right field fence, and his shot impressed not only our coaches, but me, too. That was maybe the first homer I'd given up to a lefty in about 10 years, but eight of those 10 years I was in retirement. If you look at my stats, I'd probably be one of the best pitchers you could find in terms of giving up homers to lefties.

That didn't do me any good now, and before I knew it, I was in a jam. The next hitter chopped a sinker over my head for a base hit, and to make matters worse, he stole second. It was time to work out of a mess, but it felt good. The competitive juices were flowing again in my veins — and in my mind. I wasn't thinking about throwing the ball over the backstop or into the dirt. I was just thinking about throwing and how good it felt to be out here, playing ball again, for real, at age 39.

I let loose with a fastball, then a slider. I coaxed the next two hitters to fly out, and the guy after them grounded out to short.

And that was it. Two innings, 25 pitches, one run, and my comeback debut was over.

It was one of my proudest days ever, and inside I bubbled with excitement. As the game wore on, I could sense everyone was excited for me, too. My slider had hit 86 on the radar gun, and that was remarkable. But more than all the numbers, I was proud of my demeanor on the mound. I was poised and in control, not just of my pitches, but of myself. My concentration level reached a plateau I hadn't experienced in years. My legs and body felt strong, and my mind was fired up, but I was relaxed.

After the game, I iced the arm. I ran. I felt strong and happy and focused, and inside, I was beaming. This was one of the greatest days of my life. People said things with their eyes. When you impress people who are hard to impress, they don't always say much. They just kind of look at you. And they are looking at me like we both know I had something.

The media knew, too. A few reporters couldn't wait to get the scoop from me after this outing. A few months earlier, Bill Gleason, our longtime family friend and a writer from the *Daily Southtown*, had called me up and said, "Some of us were sitting around and I said, 'Hey, what about a new lefty that might pitch in the big leagues this year?' They said, 'Who?' and I said, 'Steve Trout.'" Nobody believed him, but he had heard it might be true and he wanted the story. I didn't give it to him, or anybody else, because heading into spring training I was focused and wanted nothing to interfere. From then on, Bill has treated me differently, as if I disrespected him. I'm sorry, but I had to do it.

And now, after my outing, there was no avoiding the media. My return, after all, was a remarkable story, after all I'd been through. In the locker room after the game, the writers asked me what I'd been up to, why I came back, and when I asked Billy Connors to help me with my comeback, how he said, "Rainbow, you got me fired three times in this game. Leave me alone!"

Finally, one writer said to me, "So Steve, whose hands do you think your fate is riding on?"

And I said, "Mine."

Bradenton, Florida, March 3, 1997.

Three days had passed, and I was still beaming inside from my two-inning outing against the Mexican club. It was the greatest day in my baseball career, one I'll never forget. The coaches and scouts were giving me a lot of positive feedback, and today, I was juiced up for my first intrasquad game. Fans don't like intra-squads, but players don't mind them because if you excel, you have bragging rights in the locker room.

Today, my inning was the fifth, and it came fast. It went well, and I hit 90 on the radar gun again. I struck out Aramis Ramirez, one of the best young hitters in camp, on three pitches. Days later, people around camp would tell me that the player's at-bat against me was still on his mind, and he was having a hard time finding his stroke. I put him in a two-week slump.

My arm felt great, except on one pitch. I followed through, something went "pop" in my knee, and I knew something was wrong. The pain shot up my whole left leg, and after that it tightened up so bad I needed crutches. We iced it down. This injury wasn't something from the past. I never was injury-prone during my career, and now I felt embarrassed to come into the locker room on crutches. My groin area was bright red from the blood that had spread, due to the breaking of vessels. It was obvious now that the injury was serious.

Injuries stress you out, especially if you're a pitcher. The players and coaches start talking, and each day you miss, you feel you should be out there helping the team. But there's little I could do because I was on a 10-day rehab and there would be little throwing or even running. This was no big deal. I wasn't going to let a little knee pain get in the way of what I was going to accomplish.

Bradenton, Florida, March 15, 1997.

The team doctor felt the injury would be better with a few more days off, so that's what I did. I could feel myself getting better, but the coaches were worried. The last couple of days I had just begun to play long toss and do some running, but the days were slow and short, and I wished I could do more. Finally, ESPN broke the monotony. They came to camp yesterday to do a piece on comeback players. They asked if they could shoot me changing clothes and doing some rehab work. I was going to say no. Then I thought maybe Rob, an assistant trainer, would like some press, so I said to him, "Hey, Rob, what do you think about ESPN shooting us in the Cybex room?"

He waited a minute, then jokingly said, "Hey, I can use the exposure. Maybe they'll notice me!"

We shot it, and it went well.

Today, I was pitching against the White Sox's Triple-A team, and all I was hoping for was that my client, Julio Vinas, could come up so I could pitch against him. A former client was at second base, too. I heard some of the guys say, "That guy out there is Julio's agent, and his stuff is good, so be ready." I only had one inning, and my slider was sliding. I struck out a lefty and earned a ground ball with a leadoff changeup. The players in the dugout at Pirates City were extremely close to the field, so I could hear everything they were saying as well as some of the comments being tossed around quietly from my opponents, things like, "Be ready," or, "Sneaky fast." When you hear that, you know you have good stuff.

Bradenton, Florida, March 18, 1997.

Something was very wrong with my arm.

I was in the middle of an inning against the Twins' Triple-A team, and I was pitching well, while my arm was feeling bad. Somehow, I was meandering through this inning and hitting 87 on the gun. But with two outs, all I was doing as the next hitter dug into the box was hoping he'd hit the ball at someone so I could get out of there. My knee was acting up, and I started to baby it. My push-off was not as good, and that was probably why my fastball was only at 87.

Then, I made one pitch to a Triple-A hitter, and my heart almost stopped. It was killing me, a horrible pain in the back of my shoulder, near the rotator cuff area, and I had never felt anything like it, a burning that wouldn't go away. It was a major catastrophe. Big time. I knew it right away. I continued to pitch through the inning because I wanted to show everybody I could handle pain. But I think I made it worse.

Bradenton, Florida, March 19, 1997.

I felt perhaps it would get better, but it wasn't improving. So I saw an applied kinesiologist named Dr. McCord out of St. Petersburg. The exam hurt more than anything else. He pressed his fingers up my armpit and onto all those pressure points he knew so well. We would meet two times a week, and he denounced cortisone injections, saying it's one of the worst things you can do and that it's usually a team physician's way of healing.

I was getting negative feedback from the Pirates.

Bradenton, Florida, March 22, 1997.

I had spent the last few days running, stretching, and wincing. The back of my left shoulder still felt tender to the touch, and I thought it could be a tear. Today, the doctor agreed with me. He thought it could be a tear, too. He said, "Let's give it a week off and see if there's any improvement." There wasn't.

Bradenton, Florida, March 30, 1997.

The eeriest feeling came over me when I went to the park and hardly anyone was there. All the teams had gone to their respective sites, and only about 15 guys remained, the ones who were nursing injuries. During my career, I'd never stayed in the spring training quarters longer than the time it took to get ready for the season. Being here now didn't feel good. I felt like I didn't quite make it, like I didn't get where I wanted to be.

When the injury happened, I knew at that time I wasn't going to heal up. I couldn't throw the baseball five feet. Now I realize it just wasn't meant to be. I guess we're all where we are because that's where we're supposed to be. But it didn't make me feel better.

A few days earlier, the doctor shot cortisone into my arm, and although I didn't like having this done, I'd do anything to get back on the mound just so I could play catch again. This helped because there was no pain and I felt optimistic again.

Taytum was there at the end of her spring break. With camp resembling a ghost town, we were taking grounders and loving it. I threw her some ground balls, and she was making all the plays. Watching her move so gracefully made my injury not hurt so much.

These are the times I miss the things I can't do with her because of the separation. This is what I have to deal with, but I try to do the best I can and give her my time and attention every second I am with her. The time away I can't change, but the time with her is our time. As I think about the past, it hurts, that I missed out on a lot of her life, but I look at this time we have, instead of the time we lost.

As the season openers came and went, I stuck around, praying and hoping that my body would rejuvenate itself, but no go. I felt the tension of the coaches and some players, that my welcome was overstayed. The Pirates said thanks for everything, but it didn't look like it was going to work out. I left without much fanfare.

Munster, Indiana, January 12, 1998.
More than nine months have passed since my springtime in Florida. The sportswriters who interviewed Steve Trout will remember him as the old guy who tried to make a comeback but his arm and knee gave out, so he missed his chance at earning those big 1990s dollars. Yes, I had "failed" in spring training. My action was limited, and not only did I injure my knee, but my rotator cuff, too. My impact on the Pittsburgh Pirates 1997 season was like a raindrop in the ocean.

But that's not why I went. I didn't go to spring training for money or fame or just for something to do. I went because I decided to go. It was important for me to realize I was making the choice to go back to the game, unlike when you are drafted. That's when the game chooses you.

I needed to go. When I got there, I threw myself completely into the symphony of ball into leather and chatter into spring air. I was playing baseball, and I was loving it. Each day wasn't a nightmare waiting to happen; it was an opportunity to share a few moments with the game I love. Even though I only pitched six innings, I was well-prepared for the task at hand — well-organized and thankful. And because of that, I pitched my best every time I took the mound. My six innings weren't much, but they meant as much as the previous 1,511 innings.

This wasn't the Steve Trout of 1983. This was someone much more mature, aware of what was happening around him and ready to adapt to the situation.

When I returned home from Florida, I wasn't sure what emotions were running through my head. Pride, maybe. Satisfaction. But more than that, there was something else inside me, a feeling like the dream I had when I was being tossed in the boat on the high seas and ended up in a tranquil, beautiful place.

Now I'm very happy for the little things in life. I notice when I can make a young kid smile. I'm happy when I can know my daughter is healthy and doing well and adjusting to her teenage years. I'm happy with my own health and my spiritual sense. I'm happy to experience all the elements that a life can give you.

I'm starting to put some things to rest that were cluttering my life and my relationship with baseball. Now the more I get through all this stuff from the past, the more my love for baseball comes back. When you finally understand something, you can let go of it better. Now I can say that, if somebody gave me an opportunity to work in baseball again, I'd like to give it a shot. I'd like to either work as a troubleshooter for the organization, or directly with the general manager with organizational affairs and public relations. I would not have said that a year ago. It doesn't mean I'm looking in that direction, but the more I get these other distractions taken care of and out of the way, the more I can see myself at peace with the game. I'm letting go of all the anger I have toward the game, and the resentment I put on myself for all of my mistakes. I see life as accepting the past and not letting it become part of the future.

Even through everything that's happened, my relationship with Taytum has been a special one. When I'm not traveling, I see her five days a week. Three of those days we're either cooking or eating dinner together. We're watching a movie or spending time together playing, reading, hanging out. The other two days, I'm a chauffeur, taking her around, watching her at cheerleading or dancing recitals or dance classes.

There's a gentleness and sweetness about the way we treat each other. I'm tough on her, and she's tough on me. In ways, we are trying to make each other stronger by doing that. She has been able to teach me the beauty of being a person who is responsible for another person, and when you do that, how you also are responsible for yourself. That's what I got from her in 1984, and it's the case to this day.

She wrote me a Father's Day card that means more to me than anything in the world. The card sits on my desk, and I read it as often as I can.

Dad is always generous, always wants the best for me, always encourages me to try new things. He is someone I can easily talk to, someone who lets me be me and be silly, teaches me to experience what life has to offer, someone who teaches me to speak my mind, tries to make things better and someone I trust. Taught me to get everything you're worth, never settle for less. You miss 100 percent of the shots you don't take.

As an agent, I haven't had a big deal or signed a number one draft choice. But I have been there for her — picking her up from school, hanging out with her, seeing her develop into a beautiful young lady. She is my most important client.

Taytum and kids in general just amaze me because there's a sense of future there. How you treat them and talk to them is what you get in the end as they develop. The fascinating thing is you take that person, you shape that person and give them things for their own mind and spirit, and they grow up with that. It's like a gorgeous flower bed. In the long run, you get a beautiful array, just like children, if you treat them the right way and nurture them.

I look toward my future, and I definitely see myself doing something for kids. One idea I've had is to become involved in an International Children's Art Gallery. When you walk around downtown Chicago and see all the museums or art galleries, only a very, very few of them include art by kids. Why can't there be an art museum for children on an international level? It would serve to share the art of the world's children, and possibly raise money for doctors, food, and services for kids in need.

Or I'd like to open something called "Camp Frontier," where we could teach children the art of living and loving the land, giving them Native American values and outdoor experiences. Too many suburban kids are watching TV or playing Nintendo and not getting their hands dirty and understanding our real mother, Mother Earth. On weekends, the camp would be open to underprivileged kids and socially dependent kids.

I'd like to own a collection of coffee shops, call them "Bean in a Cup." I'd like to do a lot of things. Travel. Put together a cable TV show about traveling to Major League cities, give the sports fan a viewpoint of those places from a Major Leaguer's point of view.

I have ideas. I'm creative. And as long as I have those two things going for me, I'll be all right. In the art world, they say, "C and I or Die." It means, be creative and innovative or die. Whether you're a 75-year-old man and you lose your creativity, or if you're 40 or 20 or 50, if you lose that, you've lost everything. I've been blessed with those two qualities, and I hope I never lose them.

I think about all this and realize something: Today Steve Trout is not only a better baseball player, he's a better person. He is more mature, more in control, a person more balanced and seeking a better way for himself. The question I had when I went to Florida was whether all this growing up I had done would make me a better pitcher seven and a half years after my career had ended. And you know what? It did.

Like I told Cam Bonifay when I left camp, "Thanks for letting me pitch. It took away seven years of nightmares. It brought back my spirit." They were nightmares of me being at the game, sitting in the stands with my street clothes on, and all of a sudden, I realize, "Heck, I'm pitching today." I'd hurry up and get to the locker room. Other times my nightmares would have me pitching, and I'd throw a ball completely out of the stadium. For years, my conscience was eating at me. My nightmares were related to the way my career ended, a result of my baseball life. Those dreams were based on fears and regrets and anger.

In Florida, it was like I was a snake, wiggling out of my weathered skin and leaving it to turn into dust in the Florida sun. I was healed and ready to understand that what was done was done, and now it was time to move on to other challenges in the real world. I've learned a lot from all the hard times and have become more at peace with so much more. My life is balanced by my faith, my family and my friends.

I was blessed with one of the greatest left arms that God ever put on a man. Did I have a Hall of Fame career? No. But I know that if I had been as mature, as balanced, and as in control then as I am now, I could have been not just a good pitcher, but a great one. Spring training 1997 taught me that, and for me, for now, that is enough. For some people, that might be a hard thing to take. But I'm okay with it. I have a great life ahead of me. God blesses all; the trick is being able to find some of those blessings.

I went to Florida to rediscover my relationship with baseball. But in the process, I think I discovered myself. And by doing that, maybe baseball gave me the greatest gift of all.

Steve Trout

Index

-A-

Allen, Dick - 27
Allen, George - 17
Allen, Woody - 133
Altamarino, Porfirio "Porfi" - 78
Andrew High School, Tinley Park, IL
- 23
Ankiel, Rick - 108
Appleton, WI - 37-39
Appleton (WI) Foxes - 37, 39
Arizona Diamondbacks - 18
Arnsberg, Bradley James "Brad" - 130
Atlanta, GA - 73, 134
Atlanta Braves - 79, 81, 83, 90, 108

-B-

Bainbridge Island, WA - 111
Baller, Jay - 135
Balmoral Park race track, Crete, IL
- 104
Baltimore, MD - 14
Baltimore Orioles - 14, 36, 52, 107
Banks, Ernie - 48
Bannister, Floyd - 66
Barnes, Rich - 56
Barrios, Francisco - 51, 54
Baseball Digest - 51
Basta, Jimmy - 8
Baumgarten, Ross - 51
Belder, Don - 38
Belder, Sandy (Mrs. Steve Trout)
- 38-39, 41, 56, 58, 67, 77, 83,
91-93, 95, 106-107, 135, 139,
142,146
Beniquez, Juan - 105
Betty Ford Clinic - 58
Birmingham, AL - 39
Blass, Steve - 107-108
Bonifay, Cam - 6, 108, 149, 156
Boras, Scott - 130-133
Bose, Marshall - 129
Boston, MA - 97, 109-110
Boston Red Sox - 14, 19, 36-37, 41,
46, 63, 65, 79
Bouton, Jim – 29
Bowa, Larry - 75, 84

Bozeman, MT - 33, 136-137
Bradenton, FL -1-2, 5, 148, 150-152
Breen, Leo - 22
Brett, George - 63, 134
Brickhouse, Jack - 47-49, 82
Brickhouse, Pat - 47-49
Briggs Stadium, Detroit, MI - see
Tiger Stadium
Brown, Bobby - 86
Brusstar, Warren - 71
Bryk, Bill - 2, 5-6, 147-148
Bryk, Rebecca - 4
Buckner, Bill - 78-79, 141
Burns, Britt - 51-52

-C-

Café L'Europa, Sarasota, FL - 92
Cain, Bob - 34
Calgary, MAN, CAN - 124
California Angels - 30, 46
Calumet, IL - 90
Campbell, Bill (friend) - 24
Campbell, Bill (pitcher) - 78
Canseco , José - 61
Caray, Harry - 44-49, 69-70, 72
Carew, Rod - 40
Carlton, Steve - 144
Carnegie Steele Pitts Home, Inc.,
Atlanta, GA - 127
Carter, Joe - 79
CBS (Columbia Broadcasting
System) - 85
Cerone, Rick - 97-98, 101 , 124
Cey, Ron - 71, 84-87, 95
Chamberlain, Wilt - 134
Chandler, AZ - 74
Chappas, Harry - 34
Chicago, IL - viii, 3, 16-18, 34-35, 40,
43, 46-49, 51, 59, 65, 67-68, 77,
82, 84-85, 87, 90, 97, 101, 106,
109, 137-138, 155
Chicago Blackhawks - 18
Chicago Bulls - 62
Chicago Cubs - vii, 5, 14-15, 23, 29,
45, 47-49, 52, 67-72, 75, 78-80,

More Sports
from
The E.B. Houchin Company

Dallas Cowboys
Facts & Trivia™
by
Gary W. Stratton

ST. LOUIS RAMS
Facts & Trivia™
by
Linda Everson

More Facts • More History • More Trivia • More Fun

Available at your
Local bookstore

More Sports
from
The E.B. Houchin Company

Green Bay Packers
Facts & Trivia™
by
Larry Names

Available at your
Local bookstore